The Naked Truth!

Telling Your Story (Without Showing Your A**!)

By Josh Langston

Also by Josh Langston

~Janda Books~
Non-Fiction:
Write Naked! The Secrets of Dynamic Prose Laid Bare

Novels:
The 12,000-year-old Whisper
Treason, Treason!
Resurrection Blues
A Little Primitive
A Little More Primitive
A Primitive in Paradise
Under Saint Owain's Rock**

Short story collections:
Mysfits
Six From Greeley
Dancing Among the Stars
Christmas Beyond the Box
Who Put Scoundrels in Charge?

~Edge Science Fiction and Fantasy Publishing~
Druids**
Captives**
Warriors**

(** with Barbara Galler-Smith)

Copyright © 2016 Josh Langston
All rights reserved.

ISBN-10: 153774156X
ISBN-13: 978-1537741567

DEDICATION

For the past few years it has been my great pleasure to teach writing classes for a group of wonderful adults, folks who've lived to reach retirement, and have much more life to live. They have become not just friends, but close friends, and in several cases, cherished friends.

Many of them have expressed a desire to share the experiences which made their lives interesting. One man, more than any other I know, helped them to make those dreams come true. His name is Lloyd Blackwell, and I'm proud to call him both friend and colleague. But more than that, he has been an inspiration, and not just to me. For some twenty years, Lloyd has inspired people to record their life stories, to tell of the events that made them strong, enriched their lives, or tested their mettle.

This book is dedicated to my friend, Lloyd Blackwell. I would like to think that someday I'll be half as good a teacher as he is.

> *"Commitment, determination, a bite at a time, patience and perseverance will eventually produce a book. The greatest rewards of life require time, effort and persistency. A legacy should require no less."*
>
> **–Lloyd Blackwell**

Thank you, Lloyd, for being who you are, and for caring as much as you do.

~*~

CONTENTS

Chapter	Title	Page
	Introduction	9
1	What Have I Gotten Myself Into?	12
2	Your Memoir: Where Should it Start?	15
3	Gettin' Organized – Part One	18
4	Gettin' Organized – Part Two	21
5	It's Never Too Early, or Too Late, to Start	25
6	Superlatives – Another Approach to Memoir	28
7	Countering the Memoir's Kiss of Death	31
8	Drama? In a Memoir?	34
9	Tension: We'll be Right Back – after this…	37
10	My Memory Resembles Swiss Cheese	40
11	It's Not *Supposed* to be Easy!	43
12	I'll Have a "MAC" Memoir	46
13	Sidebars? In a Memoir?	49
14	Smell This; Think That	51
15	Editing Apps Can Make Our Stuff Perfect!	54
16	Do Your Characters Act Like People?	57
17	My Memories–My Memoir	60
18	A Little Chat About Dialog	63
19	Ho… Ho… Hmm?	67
20	The Flip Side of the Ho Ho Hmm Holiday Issue	70
21	Why it Needs to Flow	72
22	What's the Deal with Was?	75

Chapter	Title	Page
23	Weasel Words–Don't Let a Rodent Set the Pace	78
24	"You Must Invest in Yourself…	81
25	Highs and Lows	83
26	Welcome to the Discomfort Zone	85
27	Your Readers Can Help You Tell Your Tale	87
28	I Can't Forget My First Car, Damn it!	90
29	A Time and a Place	93
30	Editing Schmediting	95
31	Moving Ain't Like Editing	98
32	Damn the Skeletons – Open the Closet!	101
33	Sometimes You've Gotta Resist Temptation	104
34	The Great Skippy Peanut Butter Factory Massacre	106
35	Save Your Family's Words of Wisdom	114
36	How to Drive Readers Away–Cover Fails	118
37	More on Covers, Not Moron Covers	122
38	How 'bout an Audio Memoir?	125
39	Audio Memoir–Part Two	130
40	Audio Memoir–Part Three	133
41	Audio Memoir–Part Four	136
42	The More Things Change? Not So Much	139
	Appendix	142
	About the Author	153

ACKNOWLEDGMENTS

To all those who have shared their life stories with me
and to the many wonderful friends who helped me.
I am blessed to have been given access to your lives.
You have taught me far more than I have taught you.
Just saying "Thanks" doesn't feel adequate,
but I hope it will do.

~*~

INTRODUCTION

In my first textbook–**Write Naked!** *(The Secrets of Dynamic Prose Laid Bare)*–I focused my efforts on providing a collection of tips and techniques that I felt would pay quick dividends to my readers, and do so in a lighthearted manner. Who on Earth wants to read a boring textbook, and Lord knows there are enough of them crowding the bookstore shelves. I sure didn't want to add to that mess! Based on the the feedback I've received from that book, I'm pleased to say the goal was achieved.

My aim was to keep the chapters short and highly focused, with humorous illustrations, and to follow each with an exercise that would reinforce whatever the chapter covered. Again, the feedback I've received suggests that goal has likewise been met.

So, why give up on a formula that works?

Now, where do you start, and what are you going to write? The big question for many seems to be: Am I writing an autobiography or a memoir?

There *is* a difference, but more than anything, that difference is in the eye of the beholder -- in this case, the reader.

The conventional explanation of the difference is that a memoir focuses on one (or a few) limited aspect(s) of a person's life: my time as a POW, the year I spent at sea, my vacation on Mars, life with Donald Duck, etc. On the other hand, an autobiography is generally thought of as a chronological recounting of an entire life.

When you boil it all down, what it's really about is removing the mask(s) and revealing at least a part of yourself to the world. Diary of a Ninja might make a good title for a novel, but I suspect the real thing wouldn't happen. Why? Well, because... ninja. C'mon, geez.

For some people, the essential part of their life is the *end product* of their existence. Okay then, how does that jibe with the explanation above? Short answer: it doesn't. The more important answer, I believe (with apologies to any library science majors who might find this frustrating), is that it doesn't matter what you call it. I'd strongly suggest, however, that you make the distinction in or near your title. Or at the very least, on the back cover.

So, if you're writing about your life as an art critic, your title might run along the lines of **No Paint, No Pain -- How I Skewered Art, Without Letting Art Skewer Me**. An instant bestseller? Probably not. But at least readers will have an idea of what you've written about. On the other hand, if your book features the struggles you faced and the battles you won despite having a second head, your title might read something like **Conversations With Myself -- Two Heads Aren't Always Better Than One**.

Some readers may think this whole topic is just silly, not worth the energy required to think about it. And yet I know quite a few folks who worry not just about this, but whether their story should be titled in the singular or the plural: memoir or memoirs? According to Merriam-Webster (my interpretation anyway) is that no one cares.

If you write a memoir about your life as a ski instructor (you lucky so-and-so), and follow it with the years you worked as a lifeguard for Las Vegas showgirls (poor baby), then you've written two memoirs. If you combine it all -- perhaps: **Surf and Snow: My Life of Perpetual Pleasure** -- then it's one memoir.

The Naked Truth

Anyway, that's my take. I invite you to read on and make your own decision. The main thing to keep in mind *Isn't* what you call it, The main thing is what you put into it.

My job is to help you figure that out, and accomplish the task without undue angst and uproar. That said, a little uproar never hurt anybody.

And, the sooner you finish, the sooner you can zip back out to the beach!

~*~

Chapter 1

What Have I Gotten Myself Into?

I've heard this said often enough, along with similar sentiments: "This is crazy; I can't write my life story." Or: "I can't keep up with FaceBook, how do you expect me to write a memoir?" Or: "There's no way I can do it. It's too hard. It'll take too long, and besides, no one will want to read it."

What complete nonsense. The old adage, "Can't never could" applies here like nowhere else. Because 999 times out of a thousand, you're the ONLY one who *can* do it. Seriously! Who's better qualified to tell your story, or any part of it? So quit saying "can't." You're just wasting time that would be better spent making notes, collecting photos, working on an outline, or consulting with loved ones about odds and ends that, at first blush anyway, might be a wee bit hazy.

Other folks who quit before they've started do so because they believe, or have been led to believe, that their writing is substandard -- too flawed to be readable. "I'm not Ernest Hemingway!" Gosh, no kidding? Well then, by all means, give up!

"Me, write? I sucked at writing back when I was in school."

"I don't even do postcards anymore."

"Don't be silly. I'm not a writer."

"I can't--"

"I'm not able--"

Of all the many excuses I've heard, the one I find the most disappointing -- by far -- is: "I'm just too old." Now we're *seriously* talking nonsense. And to illustrate the point, consider that Harry Bernstein published his first book when he was 96. He wrote *three* more, the last of which was published shortly after his death at age 101.

The next time you're tempted to say you can't do something, go watch the Paralympics.

While Bernstein's accomplishment is certainly inspirational, consider also that of James Henry *who couldn't even read* until he taught himself how at 92. He then wrote and published a book at 96. According to an article in the UK's *Daily Mail*, "After hearing about George Dawson, a son of slaves who learned to read at age 98 and went on to write a book of his own, entitled 'Life Is So Good' at age 101, Mr. Henry took up reading." The retired, 98-year-old lobsterman said, "If he can do it, I'm gonna try."

Here's another thought to keep in mind. It's from my friend, Lloyd Blackwell, who has been helping folks write their life stories for years. He's taught and inspired hundreds of people *since he retired*, and he's still at it! One of his favorite sayings is posted here for anyone who wants to copy it out and glue it to their computer screen, notepad, or refrigerator -- or any other spot where they'll be able to see it often. It may seem a bit simplistic, but it's true. What it takes, is gumption.

> **"If you can write a word, you can write a sentence.**
>
> **If you can write a sentence, you can write a paragraph.**
>
> **If you can write a paragraph, you can write a chapter.**
>
> **If you can write a chapter, you can write a story."**
>
> **–Lloyd Blackwell**

Thomas Edison is often quoted as saying "Genius is 1% inspiration and 99% perspiration." I won't address the genius part, but I know the perspiration part definitely applies to memoir. It's work, damned hard work at times. But when it's finished, it will be one of the most rewarding things you'll have ever done.

And you *can* do it!

Imagine being 92 and unable to read the Sunday funnies, like James Henry. It was on a day much like today that he decided to give *reading* a try. Imagine that!

"I'm gonna try."

I'd trade a million "I can'ts" for just one "I'm gonna try."

Welcome to **The Naked Truth!** I'm going to do my best to help you do yours.

Consider this:

If you haven't started writing your memoir yet, or if you've only just begun, why not get yourself a package of note cards. They can be any size – 3" x 5", 4" x 6", whatever – and start writing down topics you think you might want to include in your life story. Put one idea at the top of each card.

If you happen to think of any specifics you want to include, jot them down on that card, too. It could be anything: a quote, something you saw, a smell, a sound, a feeling. Don't worry about format or spelling. These are tools, not finished products, and when you're done writing your story, you'll almost certainly throw them away.

For now, however, they can be extremely helpful. Take the cards with you when you travel, and continue to use them whenever an idea pops into your head. Eventually, you'll be able to shuffle the cards into some sort of order that makes sense to you. Then you can use them to manage and/or plan what you work on.

In later chapters, when I refer to such cards, you'll know what I'm talking about.

~*~

Chapter 2
Your Memoir: Where Should it Start?

Tough question. And you thought the toughest one was whether or not to attempt a memoir. Well, I'm proud of you for getting this far anyway. Figuring out precisely where to start can be a tricky proposition for some, and ridiculously easy for others.

The key is to understand who you wish to reach and what you wish to convey. If your concern is family history, and not just your own role in it, then an historical approach is probably in order. Whether or not you break out a family tree or page after page of genealogical charts and diagrams is fodder for another discussion. For now, let's assume this memoir is about you.

Fortunately, you're the absolute expert on YOU! Where do you want to take this journey? Perhaps your career has been unusual, or has provided the means to do the unusual, or meet people the rest of us never will. Maybe you traveled to exotic places or were involved in events that shaped history, the world, or something closer to home: your family, your pets, and maybe even yourself.

On the other hand, your life may have been blessed with a variety of influences --far

more than could be squeezed into a simple thing like a career. In that case, maybe all you need to focus on are the highlights – a magical journey, parts of a job, an amazing romance. The sum of those disparate parts might make for wonderful reading.

Or, maybe your life has been marked most significantly by hardship, illness, or abuse. More than one memoir has served admirably as a catharsis or even a purgative. Exposing those dark spots in the past to the light of truth can have a dramatic healing effect. (Be prepared, however, for some push back if you name names and reveal secrets. Some folks just can't handle the truth, especially if they don't have the means to spin it in their own favor. I refer to people of this ilk as cretins. They aren't worth the time it takes to worry about 'em.)

Probably the easiest way to move forward is to make a list of the most memorable things that have happened in your life. Write down each event on an index card with enough details to insure you'll recall exactly what experience/occasion you had in mind. Then move on to the next. When you're done, you can put them in whatever order suits your fancy. Then you can simply pick out one of those cards every time you sit down to work on your project and focus on just that.

Look stuff up; contact others who were there; dig out old letters, albums, yearbooks, memorabilia--anything that will help you paint an accurate picture. Don't worry about length, style, spelling, punctuation, or anything else. Focus entirely on getting the information down in a format you can save. There will be plenty of time later to edit the details and make it all pretty, and hopefully, exciting.

~*~

A closer look at my Memoir Planning Methodology:

The goal is to create a list of all the possible topics you might want to include in your memoir. Once you have the list, you may want to adjust the scope of the project. If you have too many topics to pack into a single volume, consider narrowing the focus to concentrate on one aspect: career, travel, kids, pets, etc.

1) Jot down every topic you can think of. Don't worry about leaving something out; you can update the list whenever you like.

2) Review the list and "score" each item with a plus sign (+) for important and/or exciting stuff, a minus sign (-) for stuff that isn't terribly interesting or important, and a question mark (?) for anything about which you're uncertain.

3) Decide what order you want to put the plus-items in. Number them or rearrange the list. Ignore the other items for now; you should have more than enough to concentrate on.

4) Start writing. Tackle one plus-item at a time. Check 'em off as you go.

5) When you run out of plus-items, go back and take another long, hard look at your original list. Chances are, you'll want to make changes and additions. Maybe a minus-item looks more important now; maybe a questionable item is no longer in question. It's just a list. Change it as much as you need to!

6) Go back to step 2. Rinse and repeat. Work the new material in with the old.

Chapter 3

Gettin' Organized - Part One

The act of creation tends to be messy. It's a rare thing when someone sits down to create something and actually does so without leaving scraps, shavings, and leftover parts strewn everywhere. Mark Twain's desk is a great example. I wish my own was that tidy! By contrast, the stuff in my computer is very well organized. It has to be, or I'd never get anything done.

If you're trying to write a memoir, your best bet is to do it with a computer. Paying someone to type your handwritten notes, or scan and correct your typewritten pages, is expensive and time consuming. Dreadfully so. Writing with the aid of a computer makes the entire process faster, easier and cheaper, even if you don't know how to type. There are ways around that, too.

For now, let's spend a little time on computer basics--how to organize the stuff you'll need for the memoir you intend to write. I'll keep this simple as I can, because most folks don't bother to do anything about arranging files. The very thought of digital organization is too scary. In lieu of it, everything they save from email or the internet goes into a generic Download file; some (but not all) photos go into a generic Picture file, and just about everything else goes into something called the Document file, which--surprise, surprise--is also generic.

The Naked Truth

The problem is that once you've accumulated lots of stuff, finding what you need becomes difficult, if not impossible. Instead of looking through just the photos you need for your book, you have to wade through ALL the photos on your machine. The notes you wrote about Uncle Nimbus and the three-legged mountain lion are hidden somewhere between reams of tax records and dozens of cat videos. Or worse. You can do better than that!

In fact, if you can devise a system for storing socks and underwear in different drawers, you can organize the files you need on your computer. I'll address both Macs and PCs; either will do the job. The issue isn't the machine--it's the operator. If you lose everything you've done on your computer, the cause is more likely to be human error than hardware failure. This is enough to scare some folks away. Don't be one of them. You don't have to be a computer whiz or technical expert. Just learn some of the basics, and you'll be fine, and much more productive.

Depending on what sort of book you're writing, you'll need three or four places to stash your stuff during development. Most memoir writers I know get by splendidly with a file for text, a file for photos, and a file for everything else: notes, research, and miscellany. How you divvy up your stuff is up to you.

When you turn your computer on, and all the start-up processes are finally complete, you'll be faced with a familiar screen called the "Desktop." There will be some sort of background design or image--"wallpaper"--which you supplied or which was provided by the computer maker. Sprinkled on top of the wallpaper are a bunch of little pictures called "icons." These gizmos indicate the function provided by the associated program. Clicking on one of them will start your word processor, another will take you to the internet, another might play music or launch a photo-editing program. You'll also see a number of what appear to be **file folders**.

It's the folders we're interested in. Any folder icon you see on the Desktop is easy to get to. Just double-click one, and it will open. It works the same way on Macs and PCs.

To create a new folder, simply **right click** *on the desktop--anywhere on the wallpaper that isn't covered by an icon. Look for the option that says* **New**, *then select* **File Folder**.

Go ahead and create a folder, then name it for your project's text files. (The naming process varies a bit between different versions of the operating systems. Just take your time, and you'll figure it out with little trouble.) Call the file whatever you'd like.

Repeat the process as needed to create storage space for everything you intend to use or include in your project: photos, genealogical charts and data, other research, etc. We'll talk about how to use these folders later, and in Part 2 we'll discuss how to move the files you already have into them.

Consider This:

If you haven't already done it, take the time now to figure out what folders you'd like to use for your project. You don't have to set them up until you need them, but it might be easier to do it now while you're thinking about it.

~*~

Chapter 4

Gettin' Organized - Part Two

**I suppose I should rename this part:
"*Fun With Files!*" But then, nah.**

I get it. Dealing with computer files isn't something any of us really want to do. On the scale of good times, file maintenance ranks somewhere between flossing and having a colonoscopy. But it's gotta be done, and understanding both how and why will make working on your project a lot easier. Honest!

Macs and PCs both provide splendid tools for managing files. They aren't exactly the same, but for our purposes, they're quite similar and achieve the same ends. On the PC, the function is called "File Explorer." On the Mac it's "Finder."

On the following page there's a screen shot of what you'd see on my PC after I clicked the File Explorer icon on the task bar at the very bottom of my screen.

And, yes, I know it's too tiny to read anything. That's okay. I'll enlarge the parts we're interested in. All you need to know from this, is how I got here (**#1**), and where I'm going next (**#2**).

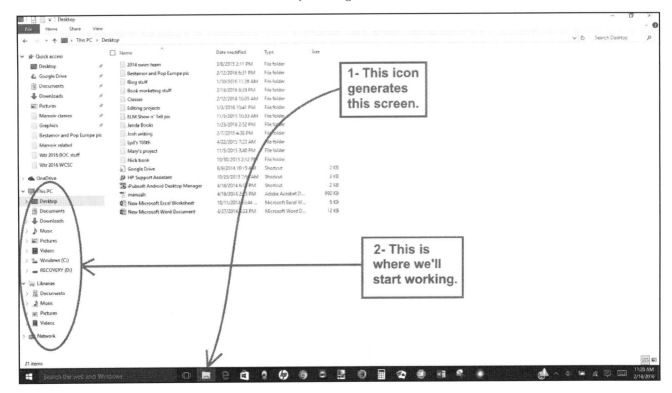

You'll recall from part one of this romantic <cough> journey of discovery, that we created a couple file folders on the desktop. We put them there because they're readily visible when the computer first boots up, and we can get to them easily--then and later.

Here's a closer look at the part of the screen circled above. The very first file group mentioned is **Desktop**. To see what's currently stored on the Desktop, just click the little arrow gizmo to the left of the name: >   That will cause all the folders and files which are stored there to become visible. It's like magic!

We can take this further and reveal what's stored *on* the Desktop (illustration on following page). You can see I store all kinds of stuff there, but it's broken down into manageable piles which are stuffed into appropriately named file folders. You can put file folders inside other file folders, too. And more folders inside of them--on and on and on. As far as you need to go. And whenever you wish to see what's in them, you just click on the little

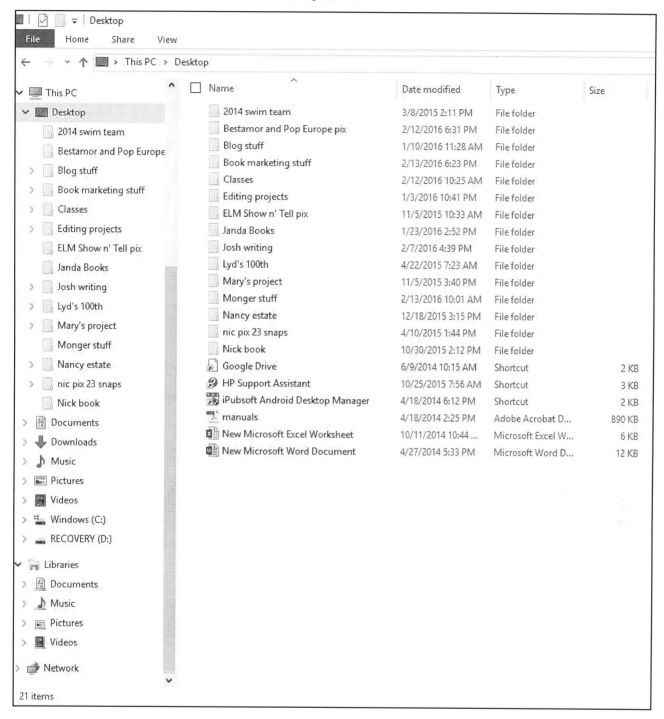

arrow. Note: If the arrow points down (**v**) then the contents are already on display.

If you need to move a file from one folder to another, put your cursor on the file name, press and hold the left mouse button, and drag the file name to wherever you want it to go. You can drag entire file folders, too, if that helps meet your needs. I tried to get the following screen-shot when the file was *en route*. And by golly, it sorta/kinda is.

Anyway, the file I moved in this effort was something called "contacts" and it went from my **Downloads** folder to another folder called **Blog stuff.** I almost got there, too, when the camera snapped the picture. At the time, the file was hovering over another folder, which is why it was highlighted instead of the destination folder. The function will highlight whatever could be a target destination for what you're moving, making it simple to put things where you intend them to go.

Okay, now it's time to go practice on your own files. Go take a look at what's in your very own **Download** folder. I'm willing to bet

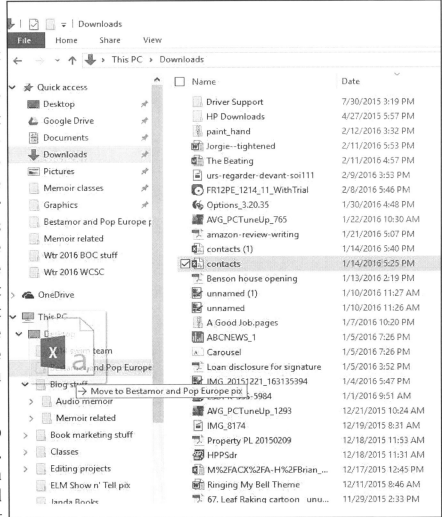

the mortgage that you'll find stuff in there you totally forgot about. I'm also willing to wager that most of it is stuff you don't really need or want.

So, why not take the time to get rid of it? Now! Just highlight the offending file and right click on it. A lovely drop-down menu will appear, and you can just bop down to the option that says **Delete**. One little click will consign that nasty thing to the trash bin (which, in most cases, is emptied automatically for you).

Be sure to search your Photo file for stuff you might want to use in your memoir project. Now's the time to move it, too. You can come back later, of course, but if you're anything like me, you won't. So do it NOW while you're thinking about it, and you know how to do it.

~*~

Chapter 5

It's Never Too Early, or Too Late, to Start

My oldest grandchild, Alexis, who had just turned nine, found a way to shock me--in a most wonderful way. She told me she'd been keeping a journal for over a year. It was chock full of her thoughts, jokes she'd heard, stories she'd dreamed up all on her own, and observations about the world and her place in it.

Unfettered by concerns about grammar, punctuation, and spelling, she launched herself into the written world--in her own way and on her own terms. Her stories may echo elements of books she's read, and her comments may not match the depth of the world's greatest minds, but she felt confident enough in herself to record them. Even more than that, she felt confident enough to share them. (So, hats off to Mom and Dad, too!) Writing, it turns out, can be a lot of fun.

I typically work with folks on the other end of the age spectrum--boomers, mostly, who all too often believe they have no story to tell, or worse, no skills with which to tell it. I wish they would tackle their own writing projects with the same enthusiasm and disdain for the niceties that my darling granddaughter managed. I can only imagine how much they could accomplish.

In that regard, there are some outstanding role models. Look no farther than James A. Henry or George Dawson. These men didn't even learn to *read* until they were in their 90's, *and then they wrote books of their own.* (Both are available at Amazon.com.)

In their innocence, children often display a degree of courage that we adults lack. They haven't experienced enough of life's roadblocks and sucker punches to know what they can't do. Instead, they just do it.

The primary goal for any beginner, should be to finish a first draft. Editing and error repair can come later. The hard part is getting the story down, and maybe not even all of it, but enough that one can sit back, breathe a sigh of relief, and say, "It's all done, believe it or not. At least for now."

Sadly, the greatest hurdle for beginners is the exact same thing: *finishing a first draft.* The reasons for failure are legion: too little time, too many distractions, too little training, too much to do, too little this, too much of that, and on and on and on. Spare me!

The only way to get it done is to sit down and write. It's not magic. It's work, but it's not always unpleasant work. Quite the contrary. And it certainly doesn't have to be done all in one sitting. Or ten, Or a thousand, for that matter. But it does require dedication and a belief that what is being written is worthy of being read. That applies to writing in the broadest sense--memoir and fiction, of course, but all that other stuff, too.

So, if my 9-year-old granddaughter can do it, and if at least two gentlemen in their 90's can start doing it, there ought to be hope for the rest of us. We can tell our stories, write our memoirs, record our jokes and recipes and poems. We can make a statement.

We are writers.

Consider This:

Take a moment to think about your own childhood writing. Did you love it, or hate it? Were school writing projects dreaded, or did you like the idea of sharing your summer activities? High school term papers introduced many of us to "formal" writing. I hated that part, but I got a kick out of making up stories and poems. How 'bout you?

~*~

Chapter 6
Superlatives: Another Approach to Memoir

Anyone who's taken a creative writing course has likely been assigned the task of relating their most embarrassing moment. For the non-writers, the opportunity probably occurred during an evening with friends or at a younger age, at a sleepover or maybe as part of a campfire gathering. Back in the Stoned Age we called such confabs "bull sessions." Quaint, no?

The thing is, for just about everyone who's ever lived, figuring out which of your life's embarrassing moments ranked as the "worst" ("most"?) could be damned tricky. I can recall a double handful of events which left me looking, feeling, or acting hopelessly stupid. Should I catalog them all? Maybe go for the Top Ten? Hm.

Embarrassment isn't normally what most folks have in mind when discussing "superlatives." But let's include it anyway. Chances are, a number of related issues made those particular episodes especially embarrassing. Maybe if we take the time to examine them, we'll find other material to include in our life story.

Strangest -- Here's a category that could take some memoirs straight off the rails, and unless your life reads like a mystery or an urban fantasy, you may not have much to work with here. But don't dismiss the category too quickly. There's likely some good stuff lurking just beneath the surface of your "easy" memories. Dig a little to find it.

Scariest -- Although this might overlap the "Strange" category a bit, it's worth thinking about. I'm guessing there were a multitude of frights in your life. There were in mine!

Proudest -- C'mon, your memory bank ought to be chock-a-block full with this one --whether the pride is for yourself, your significant other, your kids, your organization, or that time you lost 20 pounds and kept it off!

Most confusing -- Overcoming confusion about something that's immensely personal can have life-changing implications. It could be confusion over one's ultimate goals, life direction, sexual orientation, or something else equally profound. These should never be the hard ones to define.

The same would certainly apply to many of the usual "superlatives":

Happiest -- This ought to be the category with the most entries, and choosing just one would be a terrible waste. Revel in the good times!

Saddest -- If only this state occurred in reverse proportion to happiness, we'd all be better off. Alas, that usually isn't the way the world works. So you might as well cover the lows along with the highs.

Certainly, there are other "superlatives" one might include. I suspect there are people running around loose for whom the list of "really stupid things I've done" would would fill an entire volume.

As always, your mileage may vary.

> ### *Consider This:*
>
> *Work your way through the alphabet and think of a superlative for each letter: A for angriest, B for bitterest, C for clumsiest, etc. If you can't find a word for every letter–X could be tricky–move on. Then see if any of those words act as a memory trigger. Keep your note cards handy; you may need to add a few items!*

~*~

Chapter 7

Countering the Memoir's Kiss of Death

When talking to my students and/or clients about their memoirs, I notice we all tend to avoid the 800-pound gorilla in the garret: boredom. Sadly, far too many of the memoirs being produced today suffer from this condition. <u>They just aren't terribly interesting</u>.

The really sad thing is, it's not the life story that's boring so much as it is the written record of it. Too many people jump into the writing and assume that the only way to approach the project is chronological. They then cough up their version of events in a way that's almost guaranteed to put most readers to sleep.

Is there a cure? And if so, what is it?

It's the same cure fiction writers have been using for millennia, or longer, if you count verbal tradition. The cure is good storytelling. That means several things, not the least of which is tension. (More about that soon.)

Good storytellers give their readers and/or listeners enough description to make even the strangest environments feel natural. Log cabins, for instance, aren't just crude, drafty old buildings bereft of plumbing and other creature comforts. They're structures built with logs, mud, blood, sweat, and almost certainly, tears. The furnishings could be anything from clutter to cultured; the shuttered windows may or may not have had any glass, and the ancestors who lived there may not have had too many qualms about sharing heated space with livestock, prized or not. Making such settings come alive isn't as difficult as one might think. What it requires is imagination.

But "Wait!" you're tempted to say. *Imagination in a memoir?* Isn't that cheating? Isn't that like dipping your brush in the paint jar labeled "fiction?"

No, not at all! What's required is a close look at the story being told in order to find the bits that need color. Or more specifically, the bits that need amplification--the sensory bits. If you make the words you paint with more exciting, it stands to reason that the writing itself will become more exciting.

But that's not all. The memoir writer who truly wants to avoid penning something boring needs to be picky about the specific parts of the story to relate. If you've ever skipped over passages in a book, or thought a scene in a film or TV show dragged, you'll have an idea about the parts to gloss over or ignore. If nothing unusual happened, then for everyone's sake, leave it out! Or, lump it all together in one, short throw-away paragraph like: "My high school career was as exciting as a yearbook from a school no one's heard of--it's not worth discussing."

On the other hand, if the high school years were the best of your life, then revel in 'em! Put the emphasis right there. The same goes for the other interesting chapters in your life. Focus on those where something happened. Imagine trying to read a novel that had no action scenes. (Seriously? Ick. Why bother?)

Further, just as there are good and bad characters in fictio.
characters in real life--your life, for instance. When you're talk.
it to your readers to bring those folks to life. Don't stint on the
difference. And, chances are, many of those details are sensory. L

Sadly, I've run outta time, space and steam for this section. We'll dea
of tension in the next chapter. Isn't the suspense killin' ya?

Consider this:

Try to describe, in detail, the most memorable room you've ever been in. Flex your creative muscles and dig deep into your resevoir of sensory words. Let readers feel the textures, hear the sounds, and smell the aromas, as well as understand what the place looks like. This exercise is intended to help you get a better understanding of the importance of setting, but it might just point the way to creating additional depth for your story.

~*~

Chapter 8
Drama in a Memoir?

There's drama in life, so why not in the *documentation* of a life as well? We've all experienced moments where an outcome wasn't guaranteed. The concept isn't limited to sports or warfare. Who hasn't taken a test of some kind, the outcome of which would affect one's life? In my case, passing an exam meant keeping my job. For others, passing meant *gaining* a job, or entrance to a college, or med school, or Navy Seal training.

In writing, however, the concept of "drama" is too often downplayed or worse, equated with "melodrama." The more acceptable term is "tension." So let's rephrase the question: Does tension belong in a memoir?

The answer, as some of my vocal Southern brethren might say, is: "Oh, *hell* yes!"

So, how does one introduce tension in non-fiction, and more specifically, memoir? Several things come to mind, beginning with **promises**, **vows** and **obligations**. These are all common things, and many of us don't even think of them as motivators, but that's exactly what they are. We do things for reasons, don't we? Well, these can be mighty strong reasons. Add **desire** to that list, and you've expanded the whole notion of motivation exponentially!

Sometimes, the competition is just... Scary!

Okay then, if you've established that something must be done, you have to ask yourself, **"What's standing in the way?"** What is it that might keep you from reaching your goal? Another key question that deserves an answer is: **"What's at stake?"**

If my goal is to get a date with the insanely pretty redhead who lives on the corner, am I willing to compete with all the other guys who are marching toward her door? If I want to become a physician, am I willing to do the work, suffer the long hours and accept the lousy salary that precedes success?

And then there are other techniques which can be employed as needed. Let's start with **foreshadowing**. This one can be very handy and creates instant tension. And it's as easy as saying something like, "I would find out later how wrong I was." Or, "If only I'd taken a little more time," or, "That's what I thought then." But be careful, this one is easy to overdo. A little foreshadowing goes a long way.

A technique fiction writers use constantly involves tossing out **a question**, and then leaving it **unanswered**. The question needn't be as obvious as, "What would I do?" Simply setting up a situation that begs the question is enough. Your reader will be happy to ask it in his head: "How will she get out of that?" Or, the one most writers strive for: "What happens next?"

There's always the old **ticking clock**, too. How many times have we seen that used? And yet, it still works! Time limits, deadlines, final warnings--all these things have powerful connotations. Use them if you can.

GUESS WHAT GETS CHOPPED OFF IN ABOUT FIVE MINUTES.

Way back when, **Chekov** got it right when he advised producing the weapon in scene one that you intend to use in scene 2. Having things appear just in the nick of time is simply too darned convenient. So plan ahead; set the scene. The **"gun,"** obviously, is rhetorical. It could be anything, or anyone, whose involvement means trouble. Just trotting a potential threat out on your stage may be enough to put readers on edge. And that's a good thing!

Consider, also, the relative values of **known dangers versus unknown dangers**. The latter might seem to be scarier--what's more frightening than the unknown? But I don't buy it. I know how deadly a coral snake is. If one shows up in my house, I'm moving. I won't necessarily do that for something strange that crawls in. It could be benign. Which would bother you more, a black spider or a black widow spider?

In most cases it's easier to generate **dramatic tension** in fiction. Probably the easiest way is to give readers information which a character in the story *doesn't* have. For instance, in "Romeo and Juliet," Romeo finds Juliet *apparently* dead. The audience knows she's NOT dead, but Romeo doesn't. They go nuts wanting him to wait just a little while so his one great love will wake up, and everything will be rosy again. They then agonize as Romeo takes his own life, knowing it's all for nothing. Thus Shakespeare generated a level of tension that's amost unbearable. 450 years after the Bard's effort, the same gut-wrenching drama moved countless patrons of "West Side Story."

In the wonderful world of writing, stories revolve around a simple formula, the acronym for which is **MAC--Motive, Action, Consequence**. I talk about it at length in chapter 12. It works for both fiction and non-fiction. It also requires that the writer strike a **balance between action and anticipation**. In fiction, readers need a break; much like the characters they're reading about, they need time to rest and recuperate before the next great challenge arises. Similarly, readers of memoir need time to process. While they're busy doing that, you can be setting up the next bit of tension which, hopefully, will pull them toward the next episode of your life.

"What happens next?" Man, what a great question!

> ## *Consider This:*
> ***In crafting your story, try to find a way to break the narrative so that at least one essential question remains unanswered at the end of every chapter.***

~*~

Chapter 9
Tension: We'll be Right Back, after this . . .

Tension is (or should be) a writer's stock in trade. It's what causes readers to stay up late to "finish just one more" page, scene, chapter, part, or volume of your epic--be it fiction or something else. Tension is shorthand for any literary technique which operates on the most tantalizing of questions: "What happens next?"

About the only place where tension isn't welcome would be in the directions for a do-it-yourself project. In such cases what comes next must be abundantly clear, as failure to provide it won't result in mere tension, as it will in a story, but could result in physical harm, either to the consumer or the poor schlub who sold the fershlushinger item in question. Readers rarely hunt down writers to hurt them for plot failures. (And, just to be clear, Stephen King's novel, **Misery**, was not autobiographical!)

Admittedly, it's easier to work tension into fiction than to use it in a memoir. Still, it can be done, and with great effect. Yours included. Assuming you've chosen the most interesting moments of your life story to record. Earlier, I suggested that you make a list of things to include, but in case you haven't done that yet, I'll make one up as an example:

– Landing the dream job

– Marriage

– Death of a loved one

– Encounter with someone famous

– A great achievement

– A great failure

– Birth of a child

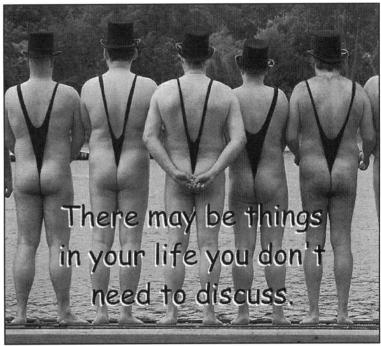

I've made no effort to put these in any order, nor are they meant to portray the most meaningful events in my own life. When working on your own list, take a moment to be sure the "big" events are included and decide if some ought to be left out. (An Inventory of Life Events is included in the Appendix.)

If you break each of the events down, you'll probably find there was a time when the outcome was in doubt--maybe competition for the dream job was staggering, or a marriage proposal seemed impossible, or a loved one appeared perfectly fine, and plans had been made, and then... Focusing on the details may reveal opportunities to present the doubts you had or the barriers which stood in your way. It might also mean you recall great expectations dashed by reality.

Relating these critical elements of your story can and should be done carefully and with the possibility of failure clearly shown. Whenever an outcome is in doubt, there's an opportunity to create tension. Once you've identified it, additional techniques can be borrowed from fiction writing to further enhance it.

Raising the stakes, in fiction, is a tried and true tension builder. What happened in your life event that made it even more important at one point than another? Who else is depending on you? Focus on that, and the tension level is bound to go up.

A time limit of some kind can have a similar effect. Fiction writers call it a "ticking clock." Who hasn't experienced deadlines in life? Was there one involved in your experience?

Added barriers work in fiction; they should work in non-fiction, too. Not only would the hero have to scale a near-vertical wall, the bad guys greased it! Your memoir need not be that melodramatic, but every layer of resistance to your success offers a means to crank up the tension level in your life's story.

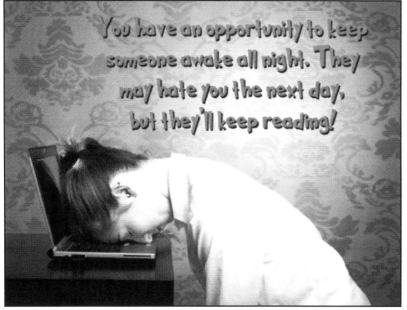

See if you can find more than one way a failure might impact you: physically, emotionally, or psychologically. Getting all three amounts to the trifecta of tension.

If you're writing non-fiction, and especially if you're working on a memoir, you should take every opportunity available to create and maintain tension in your work. It can be hard, and sometimes nearly impossible, but it will be worth it in the end.

I promise.

Consider This:

Maybe what you need is a very simple chart. Two columns should do it. In the first one, jot down the goal or desired outcome of an event. In the second column, list everything that stood in the way. The more obstacles, the better. Remember to cover those roadblocks when you write up the episode. Remember, too, that readers care more for how you handled the barriers than they do about your success or failure to triumph over them.

~*~

Chapter 10

My Memory Resembles Swiss Cheese...

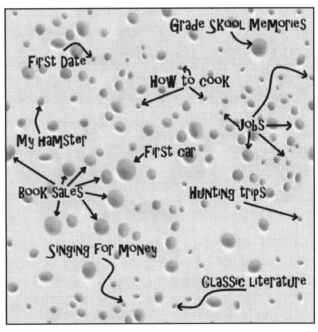

The bigger the memory, the bigger the hole. Or, maybe it's the better the memory, the bigger the hole. That's not really the issue. It's more of a "which hole represents what" kinda thing. I've no problem with stuff I can remember, my problem is with the stuff I can't remember. Double-check the photo. See all the undocumented holes? Those are the ones I'm talkin' about.

And, if the Swiss cheese analogy is just too... well... cheesy, consider an alternative. My memory map probably looks more like the Great Plains in the 1600s, shortly after a half zillion bison stormed through. Sorta flat. And pretty thoroughly mulched. Probably smelly, too. So how is one supposed to scrape up enough memories there to build a memoir? How do we remember what we've forgotten?

Conundrum. How does one get anywhere from nowhere? I posed this question to one of my classes and asked them to come up with a list of things someone might have forgotten. Each student contributed five, and I merged their efforts into one big list.

There were surprisingly few duplicates, probably 'cause I listed most of the easy ones in my examples. (Rank has its privileges, right?) Anyway, my loyal followers came up with some gems, and I present their suggestions to the world of memory challenged memoir writers. I hope the items on the list will spark some recollections of things you quit thinking about long ago.

And, if this list causes you to think of still other items I can include next time around, won't you please take the time to note them in a comment on my blog (**JoshLangston.com**)? I welcome any and all input.

Herewith, then, an incomplete and hopefully soon-to-be expanded list of things a memoir writer might've forgotten about (in no particular order). Do you remember:

* The first time you kissed someone you weren't related to?
* Being lost somewhere, at any age?
* The day your sister or brother was born?
* What really went on at Girl (or Boy) Scout camp?
* Your first visit to an outhouse?
* The first meal you cooked for your spouse?
* The first time a world event shook your life?
* Preparing for your first day of school?

* Stupid graduation stunts?
* The first time you tasted popcorn?
* Visiting a deserted house, or one that should have been?
* The first time you tasted beer?
* Something you did that you never, ever wanted your parents to hear about?
* What you hated the most about your first job?

* The first time you went somewhere you weren't supposed to go?
* The first time you hurt yourself doing something stupid?
* Moving to a new home?
* The person you never dated, but always wanted to?
* The first movie star or musician you fell in love with?
* Learning to drive?
* Breaking the rabbit ears on the TV when you tried to adjust them?
* Sneaking into a drive-in movie in the trunk of someone's car?
* Discovering that the "show" you bought tickets for wasn't quite what you thought it would be?
* When you borrowed something without permission, and it got damaged?
* The first time you rode a horse?
* The time you wanted desperately to impress someone, and made a fool of yourself?
* Seeing the ocean for the first time?
* The first time someone you loved or respected deeply disappointed you?
* Your first trip to the dentist?
* Learning to read?
* Something that scared you at the circus?
* The first time you realized that something you firmly believed in simply wasn't true?
* The "not so proper" things that went on after closing at the "ever so proper" place where you worked?
* The last thing you loaned to someone that was never returned?
* The person to whom you'd most like to apologize?

That's enough for now, but it's an interesting exercise. If you can't find some long-lost memories in this list, you're just not trying hard enough!

~*~

Chapter 11
It's Not *Supposed* to be Easy!

Writing is easy. Writing *well* is hard. It takes concentration, discipline, and attention to detail. More than anything else, it takes time. It doesn't matter if what you're doing is fiction or non-fiction, feature or fantasy. Anything that *can* be written has almost certainly been written poorly. But not everything that can be written has been written well. And there's the challenge.

Technical writing is often cited as the most tedious of all written work, yet I've done software documentation that was actually quite readable. At some hideous moment in the darkest annals of technical writing history, someone -- probably an overpaid, middle management type -- decided that "serious" and "professional" were synonymous with "boring." Engineers and software designers, it was decreed, must not be allowed to add humor, sarcasm, or even rhyming words to their written work lest it be perceived as something less than the scientific version of holy writ. What utter crap. If it's worth writing, it's worth writing well.

One might argue that scientific types, engineering types and others of a serious and/or scholarly mindset, are rarely capable of writing anything in a lighthearted

manner. But that's absurd. The ability to think clearly and rationally doesn't preclude the ability to see the humor in everyday life, or anything else. Why must the difficulty of the subject matter relieve the person writing about it to slack off? Why can't the writing be as worthy as the topic?

Good writing doesn't have to be humorous, of course, but it ought to be *understandable* at the very least. And it must be readable. Great hoary blocks of unrelieved text composed of never-ending sentences, convoluted grammar, and passive constructs shouldn't ever be the goal. At its very heart, good writing is communicative. If it fails at that, what's the point?

Scholarly work needn't be so attentive to the subject that no attention is paid to the fundamental reason for the written description. Being obtuse doesn't make something profound. It only makes it a greater chore to wade through than it has to be. A writer's primary job is to connect with readers. It applies to memoir writing, fiction writing, speech writing, and all the other kinds of writing you can think of!

I've read humorous *obituaries*. I hope my own will make readers smile, even if I have to write it myself, which, now that I think of it, isn't a bad idea. I have no doubt that doing so will require a significant amount of effort. I won't be able to just sit down and dash off something that'll do the job. It'll take concentration, discipline, and attention to detail. It'll also take time.

And for those who might not believe me about an obituary that brings smiles insead of tears, here are a few excerpts from that of Walter George Bruhl, Jr. :

> *Walt was preceded in death by his tonsils and adenoids in 1936, a spinal disc in 1974, a large piece of his thyroid gland in 1988, and his prostate on March 27th, 2000.*

* * *

Walter was a Marine Corps veteran of the Korean War.... He attained the rank of Sergeant. He chose this path because of Hollywood propaganda, to which he succumbed as a child during WW II...

* * *

There will be no viewing since his wife refuses to honor his request to have him standing in the corner of the room with a glass of Jack Daniels in his hand so that he would appear natural to visitors.

Consider This:

Try writing your own obituary. How would you like to be remembered? Can you think of a way to give a bit of laughter as a final gift to all who know you?

~*~

Chapter 12

I'll Have a "MAC" Memoir

Okay, it's not what you're thinking. I'm not talking about a manuscript and some rabbit food on a sesame seed bun. What I'm referring to are the basic building blocks of any good story, whether it's fiction or non-fiction. The acronym for this magic formula is **MAC**, and it stands for **Motive, Action,** and **Consequence**.

Think about it. Good stories hold a reader's attention through action--things happen, they happen for a reason, and there's some sort of outcome, good or bad. (*Indifferent* outcomes don't generate any appeal, so they aren't a good option.) How is any of this different from life experiences?

Little Lord Fahrquar wanted to join the swim team (motive). He begged Lord and Lady Fahrquar to let him participate (action). They gave in; he attended his first competition, and was not just beaten but humiliated (consequence). This could be fiction or biography, couldn't it? Of course. Now, how does little Lord Loser react? Does he man up, attend practice, work hard, maybe even learn how to swim and dive, then enter another race? Maybe. That would provide an easy application of the MAC formula. Or perhaps Lord and Lady Fahrquar pay off the judges to disqualify the other competitors so that their little lamb won't have his widdle ego bruised any more. Of course, that only leads to the little lordling morphing into a whiny, toad-like approximation of a human, one who can't stand up for himself. OR, maybe LLF takes an even *lower* road-- maybe he uses his wealth to sabotage the efforts of those he must compete against? *There's* another motive-action-consequence wheel a' spinnin'....

Obviously, it's easier to spin the MAC wheel when writing fiction; it's all made up! Sticking to a script dictated by life and circumstance requires a different approach, one that examines the underpinnings of our past to find the motives. Sometimes it isn't easy.

That's all well and good you say, but *my* life just didn't work that way. See, I had to work from the time I was, oh I dunno, sixteen maybe, until I turned 65. And....

I *get* it; I really do. *Your* life was different! There weren't any motivations at all. You got up, presumably because you had to; you went to work, every day for about fifty years, presumably because there weren't any other options (friends, hobbies, vacations, love affairs, illnesses, accidents--good and bad--birthdays, weddings, celebrations, or anything else). And now you've reached a point in your life where you want to talk about it. Right?

Okay, let me get this straight, 'cause it's at the heart of this whole business. You want to write about your life even though there were *no* motivations, *no* resultant actions, and *no* consequences to speak of. Is that about it?

If the answer is "Yes," then I hate to be the bearer of bad news, Bubba, but you don't have much to write about. And I covered it all--*in depth*--just a couple paragraphs back. My guess, however, is that if you give it a little more thought, you might just find a motivation or two in there *somewhere*. Dig for it!

You had to go to work at 16? Why? Because you wanted to, or because you had to? Because you needed money for a guitar, or a car, or college tuition? C'mon! If it weren't for a near constant stream of motivations none of us would survive infancy. Things happen for a reason--it's simple cause and effect. Whether or not the reason is readily apparent doesn't matter. What *does* matter, profoundly, is how we respond to the consequences.

I'm tempted to sign this rant "Captain Obvious," except that I know some folks who can't or won't assign motives--real ones, anyway--to some of the most profound actions they take. The thing is, once you make the decision to ferret out those hidden or perhaps repressed motives, the real story appears, and those are the ones that probably need telling more than all the rest.

> ## Consider this:
>
> ***Make a list of the MAJOR events in your life. Keep it short and simple--five or six events in one or two words, if possible. Then, for each item, decide which label applies: motive, action, or consequence. See if that alters your list or your perception of the contents.***

~*~

Chapter 13

Sidebars? In a Memoir?

Sure! Why not? And just to make sure you know what I'm talking about, check out the contents of the gray box on the right.

Sidebars provide a great way to bring in interesting asides that aren't directly a part of your memoir, though they're related. A writer friend who shared her memoir with me mentioned a game she remembered seeing her grandmother playing. It was called Bolita, and while it never became popular elsewhere, it had an intense following in many parts of Florida, especially among those of Cuban descent.

To me, that qualifies as something worthy of a sidebar. But then, I get a huge kick out of discovering things I never knew before. I suspect most people do, and this is a great way to help them do it!

Stop and think for a moment. Those of us who've reached middle age have seen an astonishing number of changes in our lives. Driven, relentlessly, by our collective hunger for more and better technology, the world around us has never changed so much so fast. It's been estimated that of all the scientists who ever lived, better than 90% are still alive!

Yet, most of our children, and certainly our grandchildren, have very little awareness of what life was like before virtually

Sidebar

The Gospel According to Wikipedia

Sidebar: a term for information placed adjacent to an article in a printed or web publication, graphically separate but with contextual connection.

everything became automated. Bringing them up to speed on where we came from, and how we got here, is both an obligation and an opportunity. Our memoirs certainly don't have to be history lessons in themselves, but bringing relevant bits of history into sharp focus can make our stories more "real."

I recall seeing a man delivering ice in huge blocks when I was a child. We were fortunate enough to have a refrigerator, but some of our neighbors didn't. Hence, the ice man. And the ice box. And the little drip pan underneath. All of which seems like so much pioneer stuff to kids today. But it's interesting.

And while we're on the subject of refrigeration, another memoir-writing friend told me about the hospital where she was born. It was one of the first buildings in the city of Atlanta to have air conditioning. She later learned that movie theaters were in the vanguard of air conditioning adopters. No wonder even the bad movies were popular in the summertime! It'll make a neat sidebar.

Another friend wrote about the first time she pumped gas for herself and lamented the lost days of "full service" stations where people put gas in your tank, checked your oil and cleaned your windshield. Suggest that to kids today, and they'll assume you've lost your mind. But, I can see where something like that might be appropriate as a sidebar.

What we find interesting and worth including in a memoir is going to vary widely. One who grows up with a passion for bird watching will likely choose sidebar material that's nothing at all like what a woodworker or a coin collector might choose. (Note lovely rare bird pictured here: the greater adjutant, obviously named by someone with a wonderful sense of humor.)

Consider This:

If you have any index cards left, and you should, take some time to jot down topics for sidebars, too.

Chapter 14

Smell This; Think That

While visiting our daughter not too long ago, my wife produced a tattered box of keepsakes--mostly old letters and photos. A dainty envelope, yellowed with age, lay among the treasures spread out for review. It contained a handkerchief which belonged to my grandmother who passed away over forty years ago.

On seeing it, I recalled how she took it (or one just like it) everywhere, either in her hand or tucked in a pocket of her ever practical clothing.

"It's scented," my daughter said, surrendering it to me. I held the scrap of linen to my nose, took a whiff, and *wham!* The fragrance instantly brought my grandmother back into my life. I sat at the table weeping like a lost child and feeling like an idiot.

That's the power of memory set off by a sensory trigger. It's what you must strive to include in your memoir, because it will bind your readers to your story.

We all know the power of the senses, and we've all heard how the best writers use them in their work. "Sensory writing," we're told over and over, "is the path to greatness."

"Yes, yes! Amen!" we say, because we're all members of the writing choir. And then we go right back to doing business the old way.

Why? Because most of us don't practice *using* our senses, at least, not for writing. Our world is so visually attuned, we rarely think any other way.

Memoir writers have a wonderful opportunity to take advantage of sensory writing. Because they're relating things which actually happened in places that actually exist they should be able to draw on actual sensory details, especially the non-visual variety.

If something happened in Grandpa's work shop, what specifics could be worked into the telling of it? Did Grandpa smoke a pipe or a cigar? Were the shelves loaded with cans of lacquer, paint, varnish, or other things with a strong and specific odor? Were there wood shavings on the floor? Cans, boxes or bags of nails and screws? Lengths of wood? Sawdust in the air?

All such things can be described in terms of touch or smell, maybe even taste.

Maybe Grandpa disdained woodworking and focused more on engines and car repairs. That would provide a different array of sensory stuff. Machine tools, grease, soiled rags, and fluids of various kinds.

Or maybe you're talking about a farm family. The potential for sensory material from such an environment is endless. F'rinstance: in the minds of most people, Granny's apple pie smelled better by far than the stuff cranked out in factories. One wonders how much of such "pastry" is real, and how much is synthetic. Your job is to isolate just what made Granny's pies better.

Focus on the textures: the gentle crust and the soft squish of apple. Inhale the aroma of a fresh confection as it swirls in the air and fills the room. Imagine the sharp tang of the fruit, still warm from the oven, as it hits your tongue. If you want to bring readers into your world, lead them by the nose.

Consider the following list of smells. Anyone who dares to wear the "Writer" label should be able to conjure a way to work all of these into appropriate settings. And when they do, those descriptive places will have a much better chance of coming alive for readers:

Puppy breath **Gasoline**
A baby's head **Smoke on clothing**
Chocolate **Bacon**
Freshly brewed coffee **Pizza**
Vanilla **Burnt microwave popcorn**
Christmas trees **Ciagarette butts**
Bus exhaust **Grandma**
Raw sewerage **Fresh laundry**

Obviously, the list isn't meant to be inspiring. For most folks, however, each of these smells is wired to one or more memories, and just reading them will send a tiny surge of electricity ripping through the reader's cognitive connecting tissue to revive dormant thoughts of past experiences. Pupils will contract, fists will tighten, throats will go dry, breathing will change--and the sensory bits of those remembered moments will merge with your scene. As if by magic, your reader will not simply translate your words into an image, they'll *experience* it.

> ## Consider This:
>
> *Here's an exercise I recommend for my fiction writing students. Memoir writers can certainly learn from it, too.*
>
> *Take a field trip to your nearest deli or pastry shop--any place that serves fresh baked goods will suffice. But don't just imagine this. If there's any way you can arrange to actually go to such a place, the exercise will work significantly better. So, get up–now–and go!*
>
> *Buy something to eat, and get some coffee, tea or hot chocolate, too. Then sit down with your notepad and pencil, close your eyes, and inhale through your nose. Try to identify everything you smell--pastries, beverages, toppings, whatever. Keep your eyes closed until you've got at least a half dozen. Then, open your eyes and jot them down as fast as you can. Make sure you write enough about each one to prove you smelled it.*
>
> *Next, take a bite of your pastry and a sip of your drink. Close your eyes again and concentrate on the taste and texture of what you're chewing. Note the flavor and feel of every constituent part. Then write it all down--every bit of sensory information you can remember.*
>
> *Repeat the process for everything you hear: conversations, the sounds of traffic, noise from the kitchen. Jot it down. Capture it all.*
>
> *What you're doing is training your non-visual senses to experience the world. Your readers will thank you for it.*

~*~

Chapter 15

Editing Apps Can Make Our Stuff Perfect!

~~Bullsh~~ Uh, make that, "No." For proof, look no further than the "auto-correct" option on your (alleged) smartphone, a function that's generated more embarrassment than all the unintended pregnancies on record.

I'll admit, technology can improve our work. Word processors alone easily prove that, but we're crazy if we expect some sort of techno-wizardry to do more than help us get our stuff to the "okay" level. The brutal truth is, no matter how snazzy the software looks or how lofty the claims are, we still have to do the heavy lifting. That's we, meaning you and me.

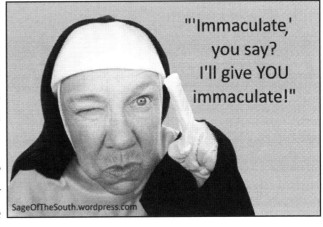

But the technology sellers are still peddlin' this stuff, and writers are still buyin' it, so it only seems right that someone discusses it.

Four programs for making writer's lives easier and more error-free dominate the market. The first is Microsoft Word which has been around, it seems, since... well, since forever. In fact, the first version of Word actually came out in 1983, which in terms of personal computing *is* forever. Nobody actually cares how many versions (sub-versions, revisions, and re-revisions) of this venerable program exist, but the number has to be stratospheric. Most of the really useful stuff in Word has been in the product since the mid-1990s, although that hasn't kept the software giant from constantly tinkering with it, adding so many bells and whistles that its primary function -- word processing, remember? -- is almost hidden. That said, the good stuff is still in there, and two of Word's earliest enhancements can actually help you write better: spell checking and grammar checking.

Spell check only counts if you use it.

Stop yawning! I'll admit, neither function is flashy, but both are reliable within certain limits, which isn't surprising when you consider they've been tested by a zillion users for a couple decades. That wasn't a tyop; I really did say decades. I rely on Word's spell checker, because I'm a lousy speller. (And my handwriting isn't going to win any awards either.) As for the grammar checker, I'm not a huge fan. That's not because Word's grammar checker does a bad job; it does what it can, but I can do it better. Still, I don't turn it off, because there's always the chance I'll miss something. What could it hurt?

I'm more likely to break a rule of grammar intentionally than accidentally. Since none of the grammar checkers on the market are good enough to know which is which, I rely on my own judgment. You should, too, even if your grammar skills are a bit on the sketchy side. So, review the flags that Word (or the other programs I'll mention) raise. If the issue merits a change, make it. If not, ignore it. But don't assume you're done. You still need someone with a critical eye to examine your work, especially if your own eye isn't critical enough. Just because something is grammatically correct doesn't mean it's worth reading. Ever slogged through a really boring book? I have. Too many, in fact, and I absolutely refuse to write one. You should, too.

In addition to Word, there are many other programs available to check your work for spelling and grammar gaffs. The biggies are Ginger, Grammarly, and After The Deadline. They are by no means the standard for all programs of this ilk, nor are they likely the best, but they're the ones currently getting the most attention. They're all clean and spiffy and promise to deliver what you want. Alas, if you write fiction, that's not gonna happen.

They'll spot clearly misspelled words, and they might even pick up on contextual spelling errors -- like improper usage of they're, there, and their. God help you if you type hots instead of host, or plumb instead of plump. (Just for fun, see what funky paragraphs you can come up with using those four mis-wordings, or whatever they're called.)

I'm disappointed that these programs don't learn from their users. Seriously, whatever happened to "artificial intelligence?" If I'm writing a novel (which quite honestly, I'd rather be doing right now), and I run it through a program whose writing rules were meant for scientific papers or software documentation, the results will be ugly. Not only will they be massively discouraging, they'll mostly be wrong. Shouldn't the program be able to figure out I need a different set of rules? I see it as an unnecessary burden on creativity.

If I feel the need to dangle a modifier, I'll dangle one. I don't need the blessing of some knuckle-rapping robot. The same goes for run-on sentences, which can often be quite effective. The occasional incomplete sentence works the same way, as do split infinitives, passive voice, contractions and colloquialisms. It's art, folks, not engineering. If the goal was to make every writer produce the same stuff, there would be no need for more than one writer.

Consider This:

Just for a change, why not take the gloves off? Give yourself permission to write something straight from your heart. Pick a subject that has some emotional weight to is, and just start writing. Let it all out. If you were wronged, spell out what it felt like. If you suffered a romantic setback, detail the effects of such an open wound: what did you think; how did you react; where did you go; in whom did you confide? The same goes for unbridled joy and laughter.

It will be up to you to decide if such soul-bearing remarks have a place in your story, but I'm guessing they will. Beyond that, you might find a different voice, one that deserves serious consideration. Perhaps it's the one which should have been in charge all along.

Just remember: if you never give that voice an outlet, you'll never know.

~*~

Chapter 16

Do Your Characters Act Like People?

Wait–You mean my human characters?

It may seem like a stupid question, but it's not. In the process of working our way out of caves and into cars, we have developed certain patterns of behavior which are common to all races and nationalities. The pattern I find significant, as it relates to storytelling, is how we respond to crisis. We've been doing it for a long, long time, and we do it the same way, over and over.

So, again, are your characters — fiction or non-fiction — acting like real people?

Need more detail? Imagine you've just been in an accident, or you've received unexpected news (good or bad), or something else of significance has occurred. What happens next?

Here's where the behavior pattern kicks in. It involves four steps which I first learned about in a blog by bestselling author Jim Butcher. They are:

– **An emotional reaction to what just happened, followed by,**
– **A review and evaluation of what just happened, followed by,**

- The anticipation of a response to what just happened, followed by,
- A choice based on the foregoing.

That may look like a heap of stuff, but taken a step at a time, it will feel pretty familiar. Why? Because this is how almost every member of our species reacts! For example:

Imagine you're a male college student, and you've just learned that a female friend is pregnant with your child. (Change the background circumstances to see how it works with other dynamics in play.)

1) Your first reaction is emotional. "I'm going to be a daddy!" Or, if this doesn't come as entirely happy news: "I'm going to be a daddy?" Or, "Wait–are you sure?"

2) Your mind will automatically replay events leading up to this revelation, and you'll try to evaluate your situation and maybe answer some of the questions you just asked. "I'm pretty sure I was in Pago Pago at the time," or "You have me confused with my roommate," or "Finally–I have a purpose in life!" Whatever.

3) Once you evaluate the situation, you'll begin to figure out how to respond, in other words, you anticipate what to do next. It could be a marriage proposal, or a name change coupled with relocation to someplace far, far away. It might even be a short, probably ugly chat with your current girlfriend. (See note about background circumstances above.)

4) Finally, you'll make a choice about what to do, and this translates into action.

This works equally well for fiction or non-fiction. The thing to keep in mind is the order shown here–it's always the same. Some phases may be more involved than others, and much depends on the severity of the crisis. But these are the steps we always go through, and we always go through them in this order.

If the characters in your memoir or novel don't follow this pattern, they're just not acting like real people.

[**Please note:** I have no formal training in psychology or the study of human behavior, but I know what rings true. And this does. How it relates to sociopaths and/or psychopaths is fodder for another discussion.]

Consider This:

Very few people have gone through life without some sort of emotional issue. If you're one of the lucky ones who haven't, then feel free to skip this exercise. (And really, if your life has been that dull, should you even be recording it? Geez.) For the rest of you, pick one of those moments, preferably one that made a lasting impression.

Then, go through the list and detail each of the four steps enumerated here. Jot down a paragraph or two, or three, about each one. See if the formula holds true for you (it should). Read it back to yourself. Does it cover the bases honestly? Does it make you re-think any portion of the event? Even in retrospect, does it feel more real?

~*~

Chapter 17

My Memoir--My Memories

Two eye-witnesses, two conflicting stories. Happens all the time. Right?

Having watched endless courtroom dramas, either live or via Hollywood, we've all heard that witnesses often interpret what they've seen in different ways.

Defense attorneys love it when witnesses can't agree on details. Prosecutors hate it. The reverse is true when a single witness sticks to his story like a pit bull on a pork chop. I'm all for anything that'll drive an attorney nuts, but when it comes to memoir writing, I hate to see writers get "the cringe."

That's a condition in which the writer suddenly becomes concerned about what dear, old, Aunt Dilemma will say, or they're convinced one or more siblings will escalate to DefCon 9 (launch mode) when they read the document currently in the works. Hence, *the cringe*. It's understandable.

A slightly different version of the affliction is based on the fear that what one writes may upset someone else who'd prefer to keep that particular piece of business out of the spotlight, for you know, just a little longer--like say, oh, the next thousand years, give or take an ice age. These folks, and I'm NOT talking about the writers, must surely have a guilty conscience. Either they did something they shouldn't have, or they failed to do something, say something, or be somewhere as promised. They broke a trust, and they've managed to skate by without much in the way of consequences, and now, suddenly it seems, they expect the injured party to keep quiet. Right? Hey, seems okay to me.

So sure, no problem. **Except, it is a problem!**

I know everyone quotes Ann Lamott on this topic, and I can't see any reason not to join her chorus. To wit: "You own everything that happened to you. Tell your stories. If people wanted you to write warmly about them, they should have behaved better."
— Anne Lamott, ***Bird by Bird: Some Instructions on Writing and Life***

Couldn't have said it better myself. Even if the memory in question doesn't involve someone's shortcomings, there's always the chance that two people may not share the *exact* same recollection of a particular event. At football games, for instance, I'm quite sure I spend more time watching the cheerleaders than my bride does. On the other hand, she's guaranteed to have a better idea of who's wearing what in the seats around us. Unless it's blinking neon or smells of burning creosote and/or last month's Catch of the Day, I'm not likely to notice. That's prob'ly what makes us such a good match.

There's no reason to fear the truth when writing a memoir, even if your truth varies a bit from that of someone else. Your story evolved through your eyes and your experience, and as Ann Lamott so adroitly points out, you own it. Therefore, you can relay it in any way that suits you. You're the only one you need to satisfy.

So, don't worry about crazy old Uncle Naboo. What he says or thinks doesn't matter. If he feels *that* strongly about it, he can always write his own narrative. But just between you and me, his won't be as good as yours, 'cause you've got me as your coach!

> ### *Consider This:*
>
> *If you've spent any time seriously thinking about your life story, you can easily recall any number of events you might not remember the same way as some other relative, neightbor, teammate, or fellow employee might. That's okay. That's completely normal.*
>
> *Now, try writing up *both* versions–theirs and yours. What you may discover is that the facts don't vary all that much. The reactions to those facts probably will, and the motives behind such reactions will vary even more. But unless you examine such things, your retelling of events won't carry quite as much weight.*
>
> *As trite as it may sound, it's important that you be true to yourself, but don't ignore the potential for "other" truths, too.*

~*~

Chapter 18
A Little Chat About Dialog

Memoir writers are often confronted with questions about dialog that fiction writers rarely face. Not only must memoir writers get the punctuation right, but they may have to fend off comments from readers who knew the speakers in question. Imagine a scenario like this:

"I just read your stupid book, Nelda. Remember that part about you and the door-to-door salesman? Mama would never have said anything like that!"

"Well," Nelda replied, "it was *something* like that. She was mad as hell; I can tell ya that much."

"But Mama would never *swear*. Never, ever. She never swore at me."

"That's 'cause she always liked you best. She swore at *me* all the time."

"Don't be ridiculous."

"Don't call me a liar."

"I didn't!"

"Yes, you did!"

This scene is brought to you compliments of sisterly love, but it could just as easily be brotherly love, or some other permutation. The point is, if you're writing a memoir, there's a chance someone will challenge the words you put in a character's mouth or the way you claim they say them.

Most of us won't have tape recordings of the incidents we choose to relate in a memoir. We rely instead on memory, if not of specific words uttered, then of the general discussion and the effect of emotions at the time.

Memoir readers, by and large, are willing to grant memoir writers some license in all this. They know the conversations aren't recorded anywhere else or in any other form, so there's no real way to disprove what or how something was said. Time spent worrying about this could be put to much better use, like getting the punctuation in the dialog correct, or something even more important: getting the dialog to sound "real."

A few issues frequently pop up in the memoirs I read from my students, and the fixes are usually simple. Here are a few things I suggest they keep in mind:

-- Give each speaker his or her own paragraph.

-- Use speech and action tags*, *but not on every line of dialog*. Content is usually enough to identify the speaker.

-- Use quotation marks at the beginning and end of each speaker's contribution.

-- If a speaker's remarks require a paragraph break, a close quote isn't required until the end of that speaker's specific comment. (It helps to signal when a new speaker is about to begin.)

-- In American English, the final punctuation mark almost always goes *inside* the close quote.

Speech and action tags identify who's talking. The most common speech tag is "said" as in *Mary said*, or *Bartholomew said*. Other speech tags include the endless array of verbs writers employ in a mistaken effort to avoid using "said." (See "Said-books" below.) Action tags identify the speaker by what they're doing. F'rinstance: *Mary paused to light the house on fire*, or *Bartholomew turned to the mirror and adjusted his cravat*.

A good mix of speech and action tags will help keep the dialog clear and interesting. A variety of techniques have evolved to further enhance dialog. A biggie in this category is **dialect**, an approximation of the way a speaker sounds. *If you intend to use dialect, just keep in mind that less is usually more.* Be content to give a hint

about the sound of a person's voice; don't hammer the reader with line after line of words chock full of contorted spellings and fractured idioms. Do so, and your readers will run from your book like a debutante from a landfill.

Said-books: The use of other verbs to avoid "said." It's a common problem. The lovely thing about "said" is that readers don't actually think about it when they read it. It's merely a short, handy identifier. When writers start substituting other words, like "explained," "replied," "discoursed," "elaborated," "pointed out," "dissembled," etc., they run the risk of slowing the pace and rhythm of the conversation.

The term said-book comes from a dark period in writing history when a professor at some allegedly highbrow institution decided that "said is dead." He then compiled a massive list of words writers could choose from to substitute for the late, lamented word. That list came to be known as the "Said Book," a hyphenated version of which came to be shorthand for items on the list.

The biggest problem with said-books, aside from damaging pacing, is the chance for making impossible statements. Consider the following:

> **"Liar!" she spat.**
>
> **"I can't live without you," he grunted.**
>
> **"Get out!" he hissed.**
>
> **"I've got it!" she ejaculated.**

I doubt I need to address these examples individually; a brief examination of each should suffice. I doubt any of them can be performed by ordinary humans.

Verisimilitude -- The trickiest element of dialog to master is verisimilitude, the appearance of being true or real. If you stop and listen to the conversations around you, chances are you'll hear mostly white noise. Short, back and forth exchanges punctuated by endless insertions of phrases like: "ya know," "uhm," "you dig," "believe you me," and "oh my God."

A good percentage of the actual conversations we encounter tend to be banal. Many are loaded with meaningless exchanges like: "how's it goin'," "doin' okay," "what's happenin'," etc. No one expects answers to these queries; the bulk of them are tossed out as preliminaries to a slightly less bland exchange. On good days.

Verisimilitude requires that a writer capture just enough of this nonsense to make their dialog sound legitimate, but not so much that it slops over into the puddle of reality. It must "appear" real; it must not "be" real. Real sucks.

It means the writer must capture verbal shortcuts, principally conjunctions, colloquialisms, and other simple patterns. Short, pithy rejoinders have a more "real" sound than lengthy discourse, *for most characters*. If one of your speakers is a Cambridge Don or a Supreme Court Justice, longer, more erudite constructions are in order. Just be sure your less accomplished characters, real or imagined, don't sound like university presidents.

Another wonderful feature of dialog is that it will break up a page. If your memoir tends to be populated with long paragraphs, dialog will add some much welcomed blank space to the page. And that's a great thing!

Readers tire of seeing huge, unrelieved blocks of text, page after page, no matter how exciting the content. The last thing you want to do is wear a reader down prematurely. It's better to string them along with tantalizing glimpses of what's to come. That way, after they've read your book all night long instead of preparing for work or school, they'll say nice things about you and look for your *next* book. Make 'em stay awake!

Dialog can help do that. Don't be afraid of it. Use it to your advantage.

Consider This:

Said-books should be given the same treatment as adverbs, adjectives and the word "was." By that I mean treating them like spices.

When cooking, a bit of spice can make the difference between palatable and pathetic. The volume of spices you add is entirely up to you and will make your offering, be it food or food for thought, uniquely your own. If, on the other hand, you dump all the spices you have into the mix, the result is going to be awful, possibly even lethal. You certainly don't want that for your memoir.

If a said-book does a better job than "said," use it! Ditto for "was," adverbs and other modifiers.

~*~

Chapter 19

Ho... Ho... hmm?

Hang on, now, before you unload your holiday blunderbuss at me; I'm really not trying to play Scrooge here. All I'm hoping to do is save you some time developing your memoir, so hear me out.

The holidays, obviously, are a source of memories from all across the emotional spectrum. Hopefully, the positive ones outweigh the negatives, but for many of us, the holidays we remember are the traumatic ones. Someone's missing, something's lost, or we've somehow forgotten something which seemed important at the time. Do such occasions deserve a place in your memoir? You're the only one who can decide that, but my guess is in most cases, the holidays don't hold too many memories worth presenting in memoir form, no matter how tempted we are to dwell on them.

Stop and think about it; most of the major events in our lives, good and bad, don't usually come as surprises. Some do, of course, and they're typically grim events which strike out of the blue, and they're thankfully rare around holidays. Those things surely deserve inclusion in your life story, but unless you can find a larger context for Aunt

Mabel dropping the Christmas turkey in the litter box or Grampa Grundy squishing Junior's hamster with the motorized scooter he got for his birthday, you may want to just skip over those things.

On the other hand, if little Doober, your annoying nephew on your half-brother's side, picked up the violin he got for preschool graduation and started playing Tchaikovsky's *Violin Concerto in D major, Opus 35,* you've probably got a bona fide story to tell, especially if you gave him the instrument. The point is, you have to make a decision about the interest value of every anecdote you include. Please don't blow this idea off; it's important, and it'll have more impact than anything else you do: pick and choose what you put in your memoir with care. Make sure it's relevant.

Here's a thought: if your life consisted largely of misadventures, make them the pivots around which your stories turn.

If you intend to focus on one aspect of your life, be it career, hobby, family, politics, a life of crime, or anything else, you must do what you have to do to keep your goal in mind. Delve into holiday tales only if they contribute something meaningful to the overall story. Winning the local radio station's contest for sound-alike rock stars doesn't have anything to do with your career as a brain surgeon. Unless you can tie it in to the main topic, let it go. No one cares. I really hate being the bearer of such bad news, but someone has to do it. <sigh> I guess it's me.

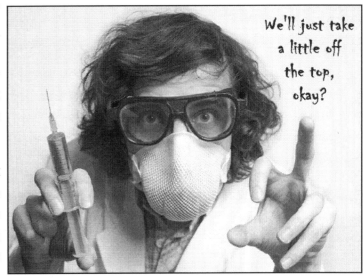

IF, on the other hand, you had a habit of singing rock tunes by that one particular artist while you dug into some poor schlep's brain, then by all means, include it! See how easy this is?

Life stories are rich with options, but it's surprising how many memoir writers miss the obvious in favor of the obscure. It's most likely a failing you won't be able to avoid completely, so don't be overly concerned. Instead, find a good editor, or at the very least, a trusted friend, who'll read your work and offer constructive criticism. More on that elsewhere.

For now, rely on your own good judgment. Don't let the holidays take over your memoir. If something happened which is truly worthy of mention, write it as if your life depended on it. If it didn't, give some thought to leaving it out.

> ### Consider This:
> *Dig out those index cards you've been so dilligently working on. Do any of them mention a particular holiday? Or is there just a one-size-fits-all version that covers the topic collectively? This might be a great time to think about which ones to elaborate on and which to exclude from your memoir.*

~*~

Chapter 20
The Flip Side of the Ho Hum Holiday Issue

Based on some of the feedback I got from early readers in response to the previous topic, and some second thoughts of my own, I'm revising my stance on the holiday happenstance issue because of an important component I overlooked: comic relief. And, since I consider myself something of a humorist, the failing hits me pretty hard.

Some memoirs deal with multiple life traumas, and a recitation of these difficult times can take a toll on readers. In such cases, relating an occasional light moment is not only appropriate, it makes great sense. Good storytelling provides both high and low points, moments of tension and moments of levity, touches of sadness and touches of joy.

Humor can provide a change in tempo as well. More often than not, life issues build slowly over time until they reach a point where they can no longer be ignored. We're all guilty of this to one extent or another. A smile at the right moment can make those difficult moments more bearable, at least in the retelling of them.

Finding ways to sneak these giggle packets into a memoir can be tricky, but it's

certainly not impossible. Be creative. Take advantage of your photo editor. With only a modest degree of effort, you can transform photos with a bit of text, add elements you wish were in the original or delete those that actually were. We'll cover some of these techniques in the chapters on cover design. For now, recognizing the sorts of things you'd like to change will have to do. Actually doing them will depend on how much effort you're willing to expend and how much imagination you have.

Sometimes just telling the story is enough. Christmas may not have been all that great after you moved to a smaller house, but watching Uncle Flapdoodle trip over the dog and spill his bourbon-laced eggnog on teetotaling Aunt Treacle just about made the downsizing worthwhile. And while you're at it, you could add a photo of Uncle Flapdoodle on the job as Santa at Gumpert's department store.

Or maybe you've got a "part-time job for the holidays" story of your very own. Some things are just too good not to share.

Consider This:

Humor comes in many forms. Find a way to express yours; it's certainly a part of who you are, and therefore ought to be part of your life story, too.

~*~

Chapter 21
Why it Needs to Flow

When we write, certain things happen in our brains that help us do what we do. The more we write, the more we train our gray matter to blot out distractions. This applies equally well to fiction and non-fiction writing, but especially to memoir.

Rather than think about the laundry that isn't getting done or the grass that's drawn the attention of the Home Owner Association's lawn Nazi, we focus on getting our fictional hero into or out of a jam. Alternatively, instead of focusing on paying bills or ironing shirts, we zero in on a recount of the day Uncle Rupert got stuck under the house trying to rescue the neighbor's cat, which turned out to be a possum. Or we suddenly forget that Fluffy was last seen in the backyard, trying to find the house. None of that matters.

Our brains learn other coping skills, too. Like ignoring hunger pangs, monotonous noises, even uncomfortable clothes. Once we're finally on task and the words have begun to flow, it can become very hard to stop. If you know the flow, then this will be all too familiar:

"Yes, dear! I'll join you in a little while. I just have to finish this paragraph."

Of course, the paragraph turns into a page; the page morphs into a scene, and just about the time you realize you can completely wrap up the chapter with just a tiny bit more work, you detect the sounds of an aggrieved spouse flipping through the Yellow Pages in search of a divorce attorney.

Fortunately for me, my marriage has survived such flows, and while my bride hates it when I'm in one, I love it.

For every writer who goes on a tear and becomes so immersed in an evolving tale, there must be thousands of readers who experience something similar. Who hasn't been so absorbed by a story at one time or another that they just couldn't stop reading?

"Turn off the damned light, Filmore! You have to go to work in the morning."

[Mumble.]

"Filmore? Did you hear me?"

[Mumble.]

"Filmore! I'm talking to you."

"Hm? Hang on, dear. I'm almost-- Hey! Why'd you turn off the light?"

If you've been through something like this, then you'll have an inkling about what a writer experiences when it flows. The experience may well be supernatural. And if not, then it's almost certainly driven by the creative equivalent of endorphins. I shall henceforth call them *plotdorphins*. Someone alert the OED!

But seriously, when it flows, something strange and wonderful happens in our brains, and it's got to be way more than one tiny little synapse firing. It's more like a whole series of them, winking on and off like a string of cortical Christmas lights--the super deluxe kind with plastic reflectors and a built-in controller to manage the blinkeration. Only organic.

I don't know what it is or how it works, but if I could boil it down, ferment or otherwise distill the stuff, I'd sure as sugar bottle it. I'd pour myself a serving every time I sat down to write, 'cause I'm already addicted to it, and I can't get nearly enough.

About the only way I know to generate this feeling is to write, even if it means I have to force myself to do it. If I keep at it long enough, the flow will show up. And it'll work for you, too.

For memoir writers, there's an added bonus, though its effect is cumulative rather than instantaneous. I'm talking about *catharsis*. Aristotle was the first to make a big deal of this, and scholars have been debating the topic ever since. Since I'm as far removed from the subject of philosophy as I can get, I'll stick with my own interpretation.

For me, catharsis occurs when the power of your art frees you from some sort of emotional bondage centered in the past. I suppose it's akin to "talking things out," either with a therapist or a damned good listener. Airing tough life lessons in your writing can provide a similar forum.

And here's the take-away: **You're much more likely to achieve catharsis when you're in the flow.** Your brain is functioning at a higher level; your body chemistry is doing its part, and the words and emotions are streaming out so fast you'll be hard pressed to keep up.

Yes, you may annoy your significant other for a time, but you'll reward yourself with something infinitely more important than a few hours of lost sleep.

Consider This:

Why not set up a chart to record your progress? Three columns ought to do the trick: one for the topic you wrote about, another for word count, and a third to record how much time you spent writing. You may have been in the flow without even knowing it!

~*~

Chapter 22
What's the Deal with Was?

...is just evil.

At some point, usually within the first week or two of my writing classes, I point out one very simple way students can dramatically improve their work, whether it's fiction, memoir, or something else. My suggestion usually generates a variety of responses. Some think it's absurd (how could anyone improve *their* work?); some reserve judgment until they've tried it, but most realize it actually *can* work, especially after I've given them some examples.

What am I talking about? Getting rid of the word "was."

The reasoning is easy to understand and even easier to demonstrate. "Was" is a *stative* verb, meaning it describes the condition of something, or someone. It's not the only such verb. "Is," "are" and "were" occupy space on the same shelf, but "was," in particular, weakens more sentences than all its passive brethren combined.

What makes "was" so sinister? It's grammatically correct. One will rarely, if ever, commit a syntactical booboo by using it. Instead, flagrant users will satisfy themselves with less interesting work, in many cases *far* less interesting.

The cure requires replacing "was" with a verb that actually does something. In choosing an alternative, *active* verb, the host sentence must often be revised, but such revision shouldn't tax anyone's imagination too severely. To wit:

-- Ichabod was tired. There's nothing wrong with that, but it doesn't tell a reader as much as it could.

-- Ichabod was exhausted. Better, certainly, but emphasizing the degree of tiredness doesn't paint a picture.

-- Ichabod dropped into his chair, exhausted. "Was" is gone, replaced by words that put an image in a reader's mind. The most powerful of those is the verb "dropped."

Want another example?

-- Jennifer was a beautiful young woman. I happen to know Jennifer, and this is a true statement, but it could be better.

-- Jennifer was a gorgeous young woman. Once again, true, but uninspiring.

-- Young Jennifer's beauty left suitors tongue-tied and stammering.

Which sentence paints a picture? Which one will readers likely remember? (If you picked one with the word "was" in it, you may now close the book and go back to whatever you were doing before. There's no hope for you. Sorry.)

The next question a novice writer should ask, is how best to take advantage of this opportunity. Fortunately, most word processors make this task very simple. Just dial up the Find option and look for "was." Go through your entire document and make the replacements as you go.

You'll find some fixes are easy enough to do in your sleep. Others require more effort, but I assure you, that effort will pay off handsomely.

An important thing to remember: you don't have to nuke them all. Sometimes "was" provides a perfectly valid and appropriate service. Sometimes it's okay to put something in passive voice. Just don't make a habit of it. Readers will notice, though they're unlikely to understand why. You, on the other hand, will know exactly why some text comes across as flat and lifeless while another sample inspires mental images and fevered reading.

Do the anti-was revisions often enough, and they'll become automatic. For now, however, try using the word as a warning flare: Look Here, dammit! Here's your chance to write something *interesting*. Someone once said a good writer can figure out how to put a surprise on every page. Why not start with the Was Warning Flares?

Pay attention to them, then do something about 'em, and your writing will improve. I absolutely guarantee it!

> **Consider This:**
>
> *Just a few chapters back I suggested you crank up the FIND feature on your word processor and hunt for the word "was." There's still time, even if you already did it once before. You've probably–hopefully–written lots more since then. If so, it's time to check it again. What could it hurt?*

~*~

Chapter 23

Weasel Words: Don't Let a Rodent Set the Pace!

For the most part, memoir-writers are new to writing. The tricks and techniques which long-time fiction writers take for granted amount to unexplored territory for newbies. One such technique, which novices can use to great advantage is learning how to deal with "weasel words."

I can hear the naysayers now: "What the heck is a weasel word? No one ever said anything about them when I was in school--ever."

Well then, what exactly *is* a "weasel word?"

Simply put, these are empty words and phrases we use without thinking. They take up space and, for live speakers anyway, fill gaps in dialog that would otherwise result in silence. In my mind, weasel words fall into one of two broad categories: those that can be reduced to a single word, and those which should be shot on sight and buried in shallow graves beside little used country roads.

If you're in advertising, a few well-chosen weasel words can be invaluable, especially if what you're selling isn't worth buying.

In this sense, the function of weasel words is to obscure true meaning while making something sound better than it is.

> "Four out of five doctors surveyed said Sugar Bombs were good for kids." Well, of course they did; all those doctors were on the cereal maker's payroll.

Corporate reports and political speeches are great breeding grounds for slightly different weasel words, but their mission is the same: obfuscation. Wikipedia lists quite a few examples. Here's a brief selection:

> "Questions have been raised..." (Implies a fatal flaw has been discovered.)
> "Critics claim..." (Which critics?)
> "Clearly..." (As if the premise is undeniably true.)
> "Officially known as..." (By whom, where, when—who says so?)

In memoirs we don't have much to fear from this weasel specie. Alas, a more insidious form likely feasts on our work, and most of us don't even know it's there. The kind of weasel words I'm talking about are the ones which look like they add something, but really don't. Consider the following common phrases:

> We started to get into the car.
> She began to think she might have lost her mind.
> He was almost ready to scream.
> Marvin felt so ill he nearly barfed.
> Katie wondered if perhaps, maybe, when the moon and stars were properly aligned, there could be at least a partial chance that somebody might, given the right circumstances, care.

That last one might actually be acceptable since it wanders under, around and through the field of *characterization*. Personally, I'd favor cutting it down to: "Katie wondered if anyone would give a damn." But then, I'm not Katie.

Weasel words are empty. They don't add anything of value. If you're writing an article and have to limit the number of words you use, the empty ones should be the first to go. The most common offenders are: **very, more, quite, rather, nearly, almost,** and **perhaps**. Try the sentence without them. In most cases, you'll improve it.

There are empty *phrases*, too. Don't clutter your prose with the likes of:

> Here's the long and the short of it.
> The bottom line is....
> In spite of the fact that....
> At that point in time....

I'd guess there are thousands of such phrases, and their only goal is to suck the life out of your prose. Don't let them! Treat them all as clichés and be ruthless in your efforts to exterminate them.

Here's a partial list of weasel phrases, with one-word alternatives:

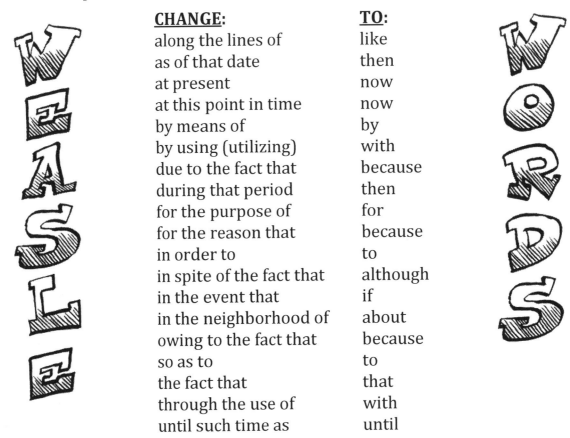

CHANGE:	TO:
along the lines of	like
as of that date	then
at present	now
at this point in time	now
by means of	by
by using (utilizing)	with
due to the fact that	because
during that period	then
for the purpose of	for
for the reason that	because
in order to	to
in spite of the fact that	although
in the event that	if
in the neighborhood of	about
owing to the fact that	because
so as to	to
the fact that	that
through the use of	with
until such time as	until

One possible exception: (I'm willing to believe there might be more than one; I just can't think of any others.) Some characters, whether fictional or actual, might *talk* in clichés. When it comes to weasel words and clichés, my primary interest is narrative. But understand, if all your characters speak in worn out words, no one will want to read them.

Consider This:

Now it's time to go through your own work and highlight anything that looks, smells, or tastes like a weasel word. If you can't find any -- *oh yeah, right!* **-- then spend the time hunting down clichés. I don't care if you use a highlighter, a pen, a pencil or a flamethrower, you must find them, and then get rid of them.**

~*~

Chapter 24

"You must invest in yourself...

...if you hope to earn any interest."

I don't know if that's corny or profound, but I'm pretty sure it's something my father said, so I'll go with profound. A determined, if small-scale, investor, Dad never bought a stock he hadn't thoroughly investigated. And though he started long before I ever even thought about buying stock for myself--50 years ago, at least--he believed his most trusted adviser was the guy he had to look at in the mirror every morning.

So, what does this have to do with writing? Only everything.

You say you're a writer, right? Or, at the very least, you want people to *think* of you as a writer. You're also the one who looks at the person in the mirror every morning, no? Okay, so the next time you see that person, ask this: "Did you write anything yesterday?"

If the answer is "No," it might be time for some soul-searching. How many times in the past week

Be thankful you don't have to carve your words in stone.

was the answer the same? If you run out of fingers on one hand while you're counting, there's a problem. Unless you were sick, or tied up with something that kept you away from your project from the instant the alarm went off until the moment you dropped exhausted into bed, then I suspect you're *not* a writer.

You may have been one, once. Maybe recently. But if you're not writing now, consistently, day after day--at least a little bit--then you're only someone who thinks about writing, or perhaps talks about writing, or even teaches writing. But you're not a writer.

I can hear the howling from my writer friends now. But if the howling is aimed at me, they have the wrong culprit in mind. Sorry guys, but the truth is: writers write.

The late, great, Harper Lee was a writer, once. And just about as good a writer as we saw in the whole 20th century. But she stopped writing. Shortly after the stunningly successful **To Kill A Mockingbird** came out, she ceased to be a writer.

I say that, because I truly believe writers actually write. Every damned day. That doesn't mean they have to write reams and reams of stupendously wonderful stuff daily, non-stop, ignoring holidays, hangovers, and hellish weather. But "real" writers work at their craft, at least a little bit, constantly.

If you're working on a memoir, force yourself to write something. Every day. Maybe all you can manage is a single sentence. Fine. Write that sentence. Maybe the next day you'll have time for more. But get that one precious sentence down. You won't regret it.

It's far easier to find excuses for not writing than it is to find the courage to actually sit down and record your words. Just do it. There will be days when you hate the thought of writing, and what you actually write may be 100% crap--utter drivel. So what? Just keep on. Tomorrow's work will be better, and yesterday's won't look so bad.

You may never become the writer you want to be, but if you don't write, you'll never even get close. The only way to realize that dream is to work at it. Every day. Don't stop until it's done. Don't give up. Don't give in. Ever.

Write.

~*~

Chapter 25
Highs and Lows

Slow and steady may win some contests, but if that's how your story moves along, you might as well take up something else, like gastropod racing. If, on the other hand, you'd like to write stuff that folks might actually want to read, you need to think in terms of different speeds. If your work only has one tempo, your readers won't last long.

So, what are the options? A story moves at its own pace, doesn't it? It can, certainly, but writers who want to be read know the value of a change in tempo. And that applies both mechanically and structurally. By mechanically--I mean altering sentence length to avoid repetition. The late Gary Provost provided a brilliant example of this in ***Writing Tools: 50 Essential Strategies for Every Writer***:

> "This sentence has five words. Here are five more words. Five-word sentences are fine. But several together become monotonous. Listen to what is happening. The writing is getting boring. The sound of it drones. It's like a stuck record. The ear demands some variety.
>
> Now listen. I vary the sentence length, and I create music. Music. The writing sings. It has a pleasant rhythm, a lilt, a harmony. I use short sentences. And I use sentences of medium length. And

> **sometimes, when I am certain the reader is rested, I will engage him with a sentence of considerable length, a sentence that burns with energy and builds with all the impetus of a crescendo, the roll of the drums, the crash of the cymbals–sounds that say listen to this, it is important."**

By "structurally," I mean the components of a story, whether it's fiction, essay, memoir, documentation, prayer, speech, or some other construct. Just as sentences must vary, so must content. A steady stream of tragic reversals, like a steady stream of five-word sentences, will wear a reader down. Cut them some slack! You don't want your readers to continually slog uphill like Sisyphus, struggling against the gravity of your tale to reach the conclusion.

Readers need breaks, just like writers. The easiest way to do this is to vary your content. If the tension has been high, toss in something light: a humorous anecdote, a lighthearted character or a moment of levity. Surely something pleasant happened at some point in your life. Memoirs can be tedious without the occasional foray into the realms of lighter material--good times, happy times, celebrations, victories.

If you're writing about a time in your life when someone made you utterly miserable, try to find something in your life--no matter how inconsequential--that will offer some semblance of balance. Surely someone, at some point, smiled at you or made you feel like a real human being. Don't leave that out! It may not have made much of a difference in your life, but it'll make a difference in the attitude of your reader. This is obviously much easier to accomplish in fiction, but it absolutely applies to non-fiction, and to memoir in particular.

Consider This:

Make a list (or use your note cards) of the major high and low points in your memoir. See if you can pair an opposite or at least an *interesting* incident to give yourself some emotional leeway. Whether you use them or not is up to you, of course, but they're good to have in any case.

Chapter 26
Welcome to the Discomfort Zone

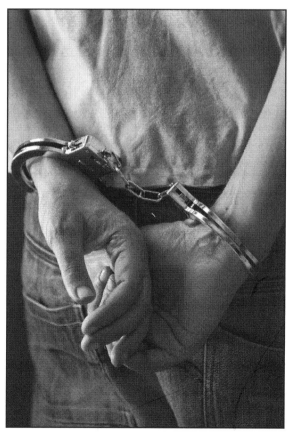

At some point while working on your life story, you're going to find yourself debating whether or not to include some incident that troubled you back when it happened. The reason you're indecisive about including it is because it *still* troubles you today. Do not for a moment think that you have a monopoly on this problem. We all share it to one extent or another. How we deal with it is what matters.

No one can tell you if that incident should be included in your memoir. It's unlikely anyone else has the right to say anything about it. But before you push the debacle into the ignore pile, make sure it really belongs there. And there's really only one good way to tell: write it out.

Tell it all; tell it in detail. Make sure you cover your feelings in depth–what you thought, how you reacted, when or if you made amends. All of it. Don't try to make yourself look good; don't waste time on excuses and denials. Tell like it happened.

And then set it aside and let it rest while you work on some other part of your story. It'll still be there when you're ready. Only when you've had some time away from the issue should you go back and read what you wrote. That's the time when you'll know if it would be best to leave the topic unmentioned. But don't forget, this book is liable to be read long after you're gone. At some point, whatever happened is likely to come out. Do you really want to pass on the only chance you may ever have to set the record straight?

Maybe you do, and that's fine. It may be more important to just get past the episode so you can get on with your life. There's no shame in that. But by writing it all down, you'll have done yourself a favor.

Don't do it for your spouse, your editor, your beloved rabbi, your dear aunt Beulah or anyone else. Write it for yourself. We all have stories from our lives which focus on difficult issues. Some of them so profound that we've shunned the idea of even *thinking* about them, let alone writing down the details for all the world to see.

For your own good, write it all down, no matter how difficult it is. Even if you have no intention of including it in the final version of your manuscript.

Why? Because you're very likely to discover, once you've aired it all out, that it wasn't as bad as you thought. The world won't come to an end; villagers won't queue up in front of your house with torches and pitchforks. Life will go on. Yours, too. In fact, you might just change your mind about including it.

> ## *Consider This:*
>
> ***Re-read those last three paragraphs. And this time, why not do the work?***

~*~

Chapter 27
Your Readers Can Help You Tell Your Tale

We are all products of our experiences. What writers, especially novice writers, often fail to realize, is that we share almost all our *sensory* experiences. When we relate something we've seen or done, our readers will run the information through a filter of their own encounters. How they react to our descriptions will depend largely on how they perceived something similar in their own lives.

For example, let's say something interesting happened to you when you attended a fair. It doesn't matter how large or small the venue may have been, because you'll be relying on the *reader's* experience with fairs to fill in whatever blanks you leave in your rendition.

Eat, ride, barf.

Certain things are a given at fairs, large and small: rides and concessions. There's also the issue of an outdoor location and most likely some kind of competition, be it livestock, baking, gardening, or any of a thousand other things.

When you mention the House of

Mirrors, the rickety roller coaster, or the dodgy Tilt-A-Whirl, the majority of your readers will know precisely what you're talking about. All you have to add is the smell of carmel corn, the sound of diesel engines, and the press of bodies to bring your crowded midway to life.

Your reader may or may not be comfortable, but they'll inhabit the scene you've set. They're working with you now, and they'll fill in the details. They'll think about the dentally challenged barker at the Guess Your Weight and Age game, and they'll dredge up a residual memory of a deep fried Snickers bar, or the gooey delight of cotton candy.

Even though we don't all have the exact same experiences, we have enough that are similar. We can augment those memories with our use of sensory details. So, after specifying the general size and condition of our hypothetical fairground, we can switch to other forms of sensory input to complete the picture.

One of the quickest pathways to the brain is through the nose. It's a short distance after all, and the effects of smell--whether encountered or *recalled*--can be dramatic. All we need to do is push the Replay button in our reader's memory. The neat thing is, readers are eager to help us. Words like "musty," "sour," "rank," or "aromatic" evoke memories that can be applied to other settings. *But the power of recall can be greatly enhanced by specifics*. Who doesn't remember the odor of cigarette butts? I can recall exercising caution when walking near the exit of a roller coaster (or any ride which up-ends patrons) in order to avoid stepping in someone else's unscheduled deposit of partially digested corn dogs and funnel cake.

Are there some oddities on display just off the midway? The "World's Largest Rodent" was always one of my favorites, even if it always turned out to be a capybara instead of a giant Sumatran Rat. Thank goodness the dreadful sideshows of yesteryear have gone the way of spats and buggy whips.

When you're offering up the sensory triggers that will pull your readers in, don't forget the other senses. They may offer powerful inducements to this collaboration as well.

Touch can be especially effective. Ask anyone who has experienced the feel of a cat's tongue, or who has been outside in shirtsleeves on a winter night in snow country. Sounds, too, can do amazing work. Anyone who has ever tried to sleep with a mosquito in the room will instantly understand.

Sensory words. Put 'em to work!

Consider This:

Sensory words are critical to settings in a memoir. Just because *you* know where something took place doesn't mean your readers will, and naming a place won't evoke the kind of feelings you have for it. If the place was important to you, don't you think you owe it to your readers to show them why?

Whether you're writing a new scene or editing an existing one, try to think of the sensory details that represent that setting. Close your eyes and think back to that time, especially if you were directly involved. What do you see, hear, smell, taste or feel? The sensory factors are self-explanatory, except for feeling, which can encompass textures, temperatures and most especially: emotions.

Let's imagine we're in Granny's kitchen. It's 1950, and she lives in a rural area. She has a wooden icebox and a wood-fired stove. There's electricity in the house, but only a handful of appliances: a radio, a fan, and lights. How does the kitchen smell? What's cooking? Can you hear the sink dripping? Is the radio on? Have you just eaten something, or are you about to? What taste is in your mouth? What have you touched? Is the room warm or hot? Damp or dry? Do you recall any particular emotions? WRITE THEM DOWN!

~*~

Chapter 28

I Can't Forget My First Car, Damn It

For months, my memoir-writing students sat through my critiques of their work. Finally, they'd had enough. "Show us what you can do," they said, in various shades of unison. So I did. The following is my answer to a descriptive writing assignment featuring a place or thing with great personal meaning.

The day I bought my first car was less than exciting. I had just celebrated my 18th birthday and thought pretty highly of myself. After all, I'd worked a couple jobs and saved some money. As a senior in high school, I managed to put most of the hard classes behind me. College lay ahead, somewhere, somehow, but the prospect didn't interest me all that much. What I wanted was transportation of my own.

My folks had been pretty good about letting me use their cars, to get to work mostly and occasionally for dates. But I still had to ask for permission to use it. Independence demanded the ability to go from one place to another without anyone's approval.

I needed wheels. And I eventually got some. Sorta.

It's hard to be humble when you're 18 and know everything.

My first car, a 1956 Ford, was only a few years younger than me, but it showed a great deal more wear and tear. The original paint job remained

How my car looked to me.

largely intact and consisted of a white that had faded to cadaver gray and a blue-green color that didn't appear in nature. Peppered here and there in varying sizes were rust spots, dents, scratches, and dirt. Lots of dirt.

The interior looked even worse. Cigarette burns in the cloth seats could not be hidden by the stains from whatever the previous owners had spilled. Clean up seemed not to have been on any of their agendas. Nor did air fresheners. Rather than sporting a new car smell, my Ford's aroma was more reminiscent of vagrants and wet dogs.

Boiled down to its essence, the only thing my car had in its favor was the fact I was the sole owner. I paid cash, $450 as I recall, plus the towing fee to haul it to my address where it hunkered down in a corner of the driveway and continued to decompose.

After a few nervous weeks I realized the "friends" who swore to help me restore the vehicle were loathsome liars, utterly feckless fiends undeserving of my trust, to say nothing of my remaining assets, paltry though they were. The aging Ford was mine, and mine alone--leaky oil pan, "Baldini" racing slicks, and vile vinyl interior included. I knew, with complete

How my car looked to everyone else.

certainty, I was on my own. The cavalry wasn't going to appear over the hill, at the last moment, to rescue me from my folly. Life sucked. As did my Ford.

"Pride goeth before the fall" 'tis said, but I had no idea it would make a beeline to the JC Whitney catalog, where parts were available for virtually anything that ever sported wheels or laid claim to the description "automotive transport."

Why buy tires when you could get amazing tail lights like this?

Ah, but what the catalog *also* contained was a wealth of accoutrements which would make my terminally arthritic auto irresistible to prospective buyers. I had my choice of an endless supply of racing pillows, flags, hubcaps, and more chrome "doodadery" than the adolescent mind could possibly comprehend. Naturally, I wanted all of it: every glittery, pointless, impractical, preposterous, piece of car-related crap I could grab.

I wasted none of my precious funds on carburetors, tires with actual treads, mufflers, windshield wipers or oil. Heavens no! I wanted a skull-shaped gear shift knob, florescent dice hanging from my review mirror (or, the spot where one once hung), a chrome steering wheel knob for hard, possibly life-threatening turns, and rear window speakers for the AM-only radio. An antenna would have made more sense, but geez, *rear window speakers*. Come on!

I even bought a gallon of paint-restoring auto wax, guaranteed to give a showroom shine. Who knew getting rust to shine might be tricky?

I ended up with the finest looking pile of fecal Ford that ever graced a driveway. My parents were not pleased. My alleged vehicle had two tires which actually held air. The others were disturbingly flat on one side.

"How's the spare?" Dad asked.

"There's supposed to be a spare?" I learned a lot. None of it good.

With my permission, Dad had the shiny pile of automotive excrement hauled away. He got $200 for it which he gave me in a bank deposit envelope, minus twenty bucks which he claimed as a storage fee. Sometimes, growing up is hard. Sometimes it's expensive. But the alternative is infinitely worse.

So, there you have it; that's my story, and I'm stickin' to it.

~*~

Chapter 29

A Time and a Place

I've often heard people talk about something called "writer's block," but the ones doing the talking are rarely writers, by which I mean folks who spend a good deal of time, day-to-day, stringing words together with the aim of publication. The condition, as I understand it, prevents writers from writing. The causes aren't physical, like writer's cramp, or writer's bowel (where one's digestive tract is too closely aligned with one's keyboard), or writer's ass where one has simply been sitting in one spot too long.

Writer's block is something else. Fortunately, I've never suffered from it. I don't know if this is a genetic thing or not, but I can almost always find something to write about. It may not be worth reading, but that's a judgment best left for others to make. I'll continue to spew out words anyway.

What I *have* suffered from, on occasion, is a lack of desire to write. That's a whole different critter, and one which I can't blame on anything else. Sometimes I don't feel like writing. Maybe I'd rather be drinking, or playing golf, or horsing around with my grandkids. But none of that is writer's block. It's writer's *excuse*, maybe, or just simply writer's day off.

The urge to take a break -- technically known as "goofing off" (from old Greek, gewph, referring to a slovenly low-life, and middle Teutonic, auf, meaning... uhm, "off") -- is well known and afflicts word merchants, brain surgeons, sanitation engineers, and everyone in between. It's nothing to be ashamed of. It just is. Calling it by some other name doesn't change anything. I believe writer's block is closely akin to this malady.

The only way I know to sidestep writer's block is to park one's posterior in a chair and resume writing. (If you absolutely can't think of anything to write about, try writing about not having anything to write about. Sheesh.) It helps immensely to have an actual place where one can do this. It could be a room dedicated to the purpose, but if such grand space isn't available, one can press a corner into service.

Sadly, even such limited efforts are out of reach to some writers, or would-be writers. In which case, temporary space should be defined. A kitchen or dining room table could be commandeered, for instance. The effectiveness of this technique can be greatly enhanced by establishing a certain regularly scheduled time when the area is reserved for the writer.

I've known writers who, on a regular basis, lock themselves in their private space be it closet, cubby hole, or tent and refuse to respond to anything but emergencies. The definition of "emergency" is, of course, left entirely to the writer. The one thing such folks aren't doing is waiting for the muse or some other mystical entity to materialize and whack them upside the head with the brainstorm stick.

If you happen to be living with someone like this, you have my sympathy. My bride, by the way, is one who has such sympathy. Alas, it can't be helped. Writers must write, after all. This need shouldn't be held against them; they have no choice. It's like an itch; it can only be ignored for so long, and then it must be given a hearty scratch.

If you're tired of scratching, admit it. Don't blame it on some delusional disease. Seriously, that's not fair to people who really aren't well.

~*~

Chapter 30
Editing Schmediting

"I'm writing my life story, and no one knows it better than me. So what can an editor do that I can't do for myself?"

For openers, a good editor can help you avoid looking foolish, and that assumes you're pretty good at the basic stuff like spelling, grammar and punctuation. For most memoir writers, the task is the first long written work they've ever done. The assumption that living your life qualifies you to write about it in a way folks will eagerly read is misguided at best. While it certainly helps to have lived the story, that kind of experience doesn't automatically make you a good writer, though it will undoubtedly help.

Fortunately, it's not that difficult to cobble something together that reads smoothly, covers the topic, and won't annoy readers--all good things to strive for. There are endless lists available on the internet which profess to warn the unwary of the "Ten Most Dreadful Mistakes Writers Make" or the "Five Things Keeping You from Becoming a Bestselling Author," etc.

Many of these sites are more interested in getting your name and email address than they are in helping you patch up a leaky manuscript. They're eager to sell you more lists and/or software so you can solve your writing problems without investing any effort on your part.

Psst! There's a special going on--today only. Just two meager payments of $19.95 (plus shipping and handling) will net you a Magic Writing Wand. Simply wave it over your manuscript, and a horde of editors and agents will storm the castle gates with offers too good to believe. Seriously. We're not kidding. Hurry--don't delay!

[Cough, wheeze.]

I also have a list of things to look for and/or change, and I suspect it's not all that different from the other 9 gazillion such lists you can choose from. What most of those lists don't have, however, is a plan for actually doing the updates. Oh, yeah, and my list is free. I don't want your name and address, just your attention.

What follows is my **Top Ten Fix List** for writers of non-fiction (which is similar to but shorter than my list for novelists). Do yourself a favor though, write the best stuff you can, <u>first</u>. Only then should you work your way through the list. Here 'tis:

> **Start with your best stuff. Then, make it better.**

1. **Replace adverbs with active verbs.** Even if you limit your search to words ending in "ly," you'll spot the worst of them. It's easier for a reader to visualize someone jogging or racing than it is to imagine them moving swiftly.

2. **Replace clichés with your own expressions.** Why re-use something trite like "dog tired" or "hard as a rock," when you could bring your text to life with originality. Why not "leg-dragging weary" or "hard as a fanatic's heart?"

3. **Whack weasel words.** Start with "really" and "very," then hunt down other empty expressions like "rather," "started to," "nearly," "almost" and the rest of their ilk. Why be satisfied with flabby expressions such as "she began to wonder" when you can leave out the fat and simply go with "she wondered."

4. **This about "that."** The word "that" is almost always unnecessary; delete it whenever you can, and make sure you don't mean "who" when you're writing about people.

5. **Break up long, convoluted sentences.** Go for a mix of sentence lengths.

6. **Double negatives are double awful.** Whether intended or not, double negatives can make your writing seem amateurish.

7. **Beware of "was."** It usually signals passive voice, and you don't want that. In passive voice, things happen to people. It's better to show people doing things. Don't tell me Alonzo was really tired; paint me a word picture of Alonzo dragging himself into bed, too exhausted to undress.

8. **Be specific.** A '48 Ford "Woody" with no muffler is way more interesting than a "noisy, old car."

9. **Get rid of pet phrases.** We're often unaware of them until someone points out how repetitious they are, and then it's too late. Learn to recognize your pet expressions so you can nuke 'em. They're easier to find when you read your work out loud.

10. **Dialog is your friend.** Long paragraphs can be visually daunting. Imagine a page or two with only an occasional indention or two. It looks like a solid mass: frightening. Break it up with dialog, even if it's internalized speech. Find someone and make them say something!

So, how do you actually use this list? Don't memorize it and try to find and fix everything in one exhaustive editing session. Take it one item at a time, and check off each one as you complete it. Go through your whole manuscript ten times. Yes, ten! Focus on each of the topics and deal with it exclusively. Then move on to the next.

Unless you have a deadline that actually involves someone's physical demise, take the time to do the job right. Who cares if it takes an extra day or two? Who cares if it takes an extra month or two? If you cared enough to write it, isn't it worth the additional time required to make it worth reading?

The number of people who'll read it just because they love you is horribly limited. So write for everyone else, too! Make your story the best it can be. It'll be around a lot longer than either of us.

~*~

Chapter 31
Moving Ain't Like Editing

I'm told this is supposed to be "art." I think it's exactly what it looks like. And, oddly enough, we seem to have a similar amount of this stuff in our basement.

...except for one little thing.

It occurred to me after spending day after day in my basement dealing with a vast accumulation of *stuff* -- and yes, I'm using stuff in lieu of a much more graphic, though certainly appropriate, word -- that I'd seen manuscripts loaded down with smoldering piles of the same thing. The difference, aside from the physical presence of actual stuff, was the volume of it.

I don't recall anyone ever using the need to move, as in relocate, downsize, or bug out, as a metaphor for editing, but why not? I'm willing to sacrifice erudition <cough> just this once. So, just what am I talking about? For reasons I don't understand, many who are new to the craft of writing feel compelled to write the way they think someone who's highly educated might write, or possibly speak. Either way, it's a mistake.

And yet it happens over and over. The need to *sound profound* usually results in a mishmash of sentences heavily laced with adjectives and adverbs that wander through the wilderness in search of meaning. Picture the Donner party gallivanting through the Sierra Nevada mountains as the snow begins to fall. That ill-fated trip began 170 years ago, by the way. If Donner and Company had followed a straighter path, and done a good bit less meandering, they might have completed their journey without having to dine on each other to survive the winter. But I digress.

Consider this literary gem:

He wrapped a long, thin finger around the sturdy handle of the shiny black receptacle. Slowly, he hoisted the ceramic vessel to his pale pink lips. The steaming liquid rolled acridly around his sensitive tongue, evoking an involuntary reaction to the South American beverage's bitter taste. The liquid was a stark black, reflecting the pale glow from the screen of his rectangular computer monitor. His concerned green eyes darted from one serifed letter to another, drinking in each word's meaning as purposefully as he drank in his coffee. (Sample borrowed from a post by Bob Dole in Answers.com.)

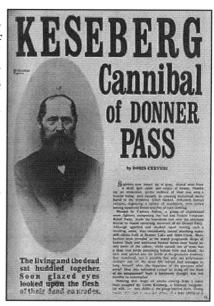

Could you tell this poor schlub is just drinking coffee while he reads something on his PC? If this book wasn't printed in black and white, I'd have put this in bright purple. (I also deal with the issue of narrative bloat in chapter 41 of **Write Naked!** See the on-line version free at my website: **JoshLangston.com**. Knock yourself out.)

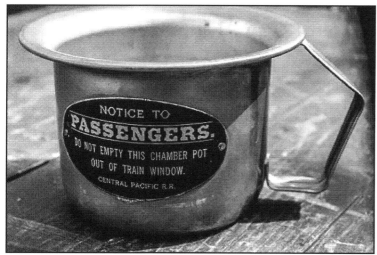

I know it's not ceramic, but it *is* a chamber pot, and the warning is classic.

The passage above is wrong on so many levels I lose count. Let's start with his "long, thin finger." Who cares if it's long and thin? Most guys don't. Nor do we attempt to hold a beverage-filled mug with a single digit. And despite an abundance of descriptors, we still don't know for sure if he's drinking from a cup, a mug, or a chamber pot. But again, who cares?

The third sentence is breathtakingly void of useful data, and yet it crawls, travelogue style, to the southern hemisphere in its journey of obfuscation. I'm guessing it's coffee, but then, what do I know? (As I'm reading, my inner editor screams, "For the love of God, get on with it!" And, not surprisingly, I agree.) Still, there's a slim chance that it isn't coffee. It could be tea or possibly even *yerba mate*. Again, who cares? Let's plow ahead.

Alas, we can't move on just yet, we have to ponder the reflection of the rectangular computer monitor in the "stark black" liquid. Someone please tell me who uses a computer monitor that isn't rectangular. But never mind, we have a more pressing matter: the mystery beverage. We're still dealing in clues about that. What could it possibly be? And if it's so vile, why drink it? Is the protagonist crazy?

Probably not, but I'm developing suspicions about the alleged writer.

Finally we reach the last sentence, which suggests our nameless drinker doesn't read like normal folk. Nay, he must examine each individual letter, dot, and tittle for its typographical pedigree as he digests the text with the same tenacity as he consumes the dreadful concoction from south of the border, whatever the hell it is. Apparently, we'll never find out.

I actually grieve for the fellow in this tale. But I take comfort knowing I'll never read another word about him.

Which brings me back to my premise: moving demands that one get rid of the superfluous junk acquired over a period of time. In short, if you don't need it or love it, lose it. Editing often requires something similar, as demonstrated. Keeping a chamber pot handy whilst editing something like this ain't such a bad idea.

Consider This:

Go buy yourself a purple highlighter pen, then pretend you're me and read through your work, stopping only to highlight anything overwrought.

~*~

Chapter 32

Damn the Skeletons - Open the Closet!

One might be tempted to think that only readers find surprises in a memoir. But if the writer incorporates some genealogical research, he or she is just as likely to stumble onto little-known, if not completely forgotten, family lore. I'd be fascinated to discover that my great-great-uncle Waldo was a horse thief, or that his step-sister danced the can-can and entertained gold miners from Cripple Creek, Colorado, to the Klondike. Finding such gems isn't easy, but they're oh-so-worth it.

But one doesn't even have to hunt down specifics to add an element of intrigue to a memoir. One of the easiest ways to do this is via a DNA test.

As of this writing (July, 2016), there are four major outfits offering DNA testing, and they don't all offer the same thing. Much depends on what you hope to learn, and different organizations offer different kinds of results. Also, you need to know up front that such testing isn't cheap. Prices range from $99 to $199, and in order to get the full range of information available, you'll need to pony up for three of the four. There's a way to reduce that cost however, and I'll get to it later in this post.

Most folks will be interested in **autosomal** DNA

testing, which looks across genders and seeks out potential cousins anywhere within an individual's lineage. **YDNA** testing is available to men only and concerns itself solely with paternal ancestry. **Mitochondrial** DNA testing involves only the maternal line.

As of this writing, your best bet if you only want to take one test, is through *Family Tree DNA*. From my admittedly limited research, it has samples from more genealogists than the others, and it's easy to use.

Ancestry DNA, however, is the only one which links--or attempts to link--your DNA results with your family tree. This is only helpful when your family tree is registered with them, otherwise there's nothing with which to link it. I'm told that's not uncommon, but as more folks do the testing and delve into their ancestors, this will continually improve.

If you're looking for general information on the source of your genetics, your best bets are the **Ancestry Composition** report from *23andMe* and Ancestry DNA's **Ethnicity Estimate.**

There's also *National Geographic's Geno 2.0*. You won't get nearly as much useful genealogical feedback, but you'll be doing your fellow humans a service for the future as this data will be used more comprehensively going forward.

Here's how to save a few bucks and get the results from the three commercial services: Do the AncestryDNA first. Its data is the most compatible, and it'll set you back $99.

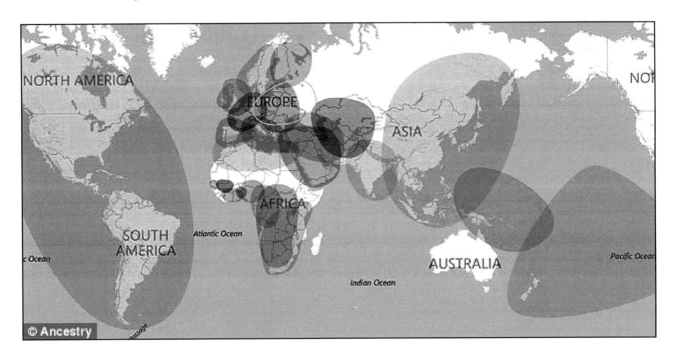

When you get your results from AncestryDNA, transfer the raw data to Family Tree DNA. That's only $69, and it doesn't limit your options with the first company. It does, however, link you with the Family Tree DNA system, for which there are significant benefits.

Later, when you've got another $99 to spend, test with 23andMe. (And if you feel a pang of humanity, think of National Geographic. They're in it for all of us, and their research is far more serious than the rest.)

Why do all this? To find out where you're from! There may not be any skeletons in your closet, but wouldn't it be nice to know where it all began? Most of our ancestors came here from somewhere else, and there's no telling how long ago that happened, unless someone in your family has already done some extensive research. For the great majority of us, we rely on what we've heard and very little else. Maybe it's time to see what's behind your genetic curtain.

~*~

Chapter 33

Sometimes You've Gotta Resist Temptation

Especially if you're writing a memoir. The trouble is, there are several temptations which often crop up during the writing of a memoir, and in almost every case, caving to any of them will result in a disappointing end product. There's no point in numbering these as they're all roughly equal in importance, and while a very few writers might be lured in by all of them, most memoir writers will only deal with one or two. (Thank goodness!)

So, let's start by **managing expectations**. There's very little chance your life story will be so utterly captivating and/or so profoundly worthwhile, that it will hit the New York Times Bestseller list, or anyone else's for that matter. Think hard about who will be reading your memoir--family, certainly, and friends, possibly even business acquaintances or genealogists in need of period and setting details. For most people, having just such an audience provides all the justification needed for embarking on, and completing, such a major undertaking. But don't hold your breath waiting for Hollywood to call, unless you've been involved in something truly world-changing.

Another common pitfall is accepting less than your best. It's ironic, I suppose, in light of the topic just discussed, but just because your life story is unlikely to be a runaway bestseller, **you are not absolved of the responsibility to write it in the best way you can.** This means taking the time to organize your content in a way readers will enjoy. Strict, chronological order might be helpful to you, but it might bore your readers to tears. If, however, the content is flavorful enough, a straight chronology might be the best way to go. Just make sure you choose a format for a reason and not simply because you didn't take the time to think about doing it any other way. The second part of this issue addresses writing mechanics. If you expect readers to take the time to read your work, you owe it to them to write good material. There are many techniques for writing powerful prose, take the time to learn some of them. (You could do a lot worse than studying my fiction writing textbook, **Write Naked!**)

Despite what the all-but-sainted Ann Lemott had to say about owning your stories--"You own everything that happened to you. Tell your stories. If people wanted you to write warmly about them, they should have behaved better."--please **don't assume your memoir entitles you to take pot shots at everyone who pissed you off during your lifetime**. That's NOT the point of a memoir. Yes, by all means, be truthful, and if someone hurt you, for God's sake, don't worry about their feelings when you recount the incident(s). But please, don't use your memoir as a means to get even. Your life story should be more than a vendetta. If that's the route you choose, just understand that when it's done, nobody will like it, including you.

Finally, please understand that **you don't need to save space in your book to mention everyone you've ever met**. That may sound ludicrous, but all too often, writers I know have agonized over whether or not to mention this person or that one, when--in the grand scheme of things--it simply doesn't matter. You're not writing an address book; you're writing a story. It's about YOU. It's not about every teacher you had, every boss who said something nice (or ugly), every guy or gal you dated, every traffic ticket you got, or every movie you saw.

Your story needs to be about you and the things in your life that matter--to you! Deciding what to include in your memoir should be as easy as asking yourself: did this matter to me, or was it just another incident? Running off to Peru with a bongo-playing socialist might have had some impact on your life; running off to Dairy Queen with your best friend on a Tuesday night during summer break probably doesn't rate inclusion, unless that was the night you met... you-know-who.

~*~

It's about YOU!

Chapter 34
The Great Skippy Peanut Butter Factory Massacre

For too many memoir writers, the task is about recounting a life and nothing more. What these folks miss is the opportunity to share life lessons from a more mature perspective. I'm not talking about Monday morning quarterbacking. There's a reason we remember some incidents in our lives and not others, and it isn't based on the degree of trauma involved. Examining those episodes through a present-day lens can help put them in a more useful context. And, in some cases, may offer opportunities for humor--an all too rare commodity in most memoirs.

To wit: an excerpt from my own life story from the 1950s, which I refer to as "The Great Skippy Peanut Butter Factory Massacre."

His name was Bennett, but I can't remember if it was his first name or his last. He lived in the house at the end of the block, but I can't remember what the house looked like. I can't even remember what he looked like. But I do remember he was the luckiest kid on Earth, and the massacre was really all his fault.

The author as a young gunslinger.

The Naked Truth

Bennett had everything: a big-screen TV (a full 13 inches, measured diagonally), no older brothers, a basketball hoop mounted eight feet off the ground instead of ten, and he had a spring board. Topping it all off, he had not one, but two junior-size Lakers basketballs, the kind an eight-year-old can almost palm if the rubber hide isn't too dirty or worn too smooth. It's not that I was a great fan of the Lakers, because I wasn't; not many people in Minneapolis were, which probably explains why the team wound up moving to Los Angeles. But I sure liked those junior-size basketballs--and Bennett had two of 'em!

When I was at his house, we could both take shots. We would drag the spring board out of the garage and set it up in strategic positions near the basket. We used leftover house paint to outline the square base of the spring board in several places on the driveway. (I recall Bennett's mom saying something about that; she wasn't pleased.) We took turns running down the short drive from the alley, leaping as high as possible and landing, heels down, on the spring board. The board catapulted us into the air and empowered us to make incredible dunks and miraculous saves. I could go from ground level to eyeball-even with the rim of the basket; I was Jerry West, Bob Cousy, and Peter Pan--all rolled into one!

Or I could stay at home. Our basket was ten feet high and our regulation-size ball was so smooth it was hard to hold with two hands unless it was wet, or unless you were one of my brothers or one of their friends. Turns were something they had three of for every one of mine, unless we were playing "Pig," a follow-the-leader game where you got one letter of the game's title word every time you missed a shot. When you had all the letters, you were out. I was out a lot. Bennett and I played the same game at his house, but we called it "Tyrannosaurus Rex" or "Duck-billed Platypus."

The other thing I really liked to do at Bennett's house was watch TV. When Buffalo Bob came on and asked, "Hey kids, what time is it?" we didn't have to listen to my clever brothers say "It's 'Captain Video' time!" which is what they always said at my house. They always insisted on using the

Look – Howdy's wearing my shirt!

democratic method to determine which program to watch. I think my brothers invented block voting. As I recall, we only had three TV channels back then, so there weren't any other choices. If I wanted to watch "Howdy Doody," I just about had to be at Bennett's.

Don't get the idea my brothers and I never agreed on anything, even though there may be some truth to it. There was one particular show we never missed. Each week the whole family would gather in front of the old Zenith to watch "You Asked For It!" with Art Baker. It became something of a tradition.

The show's sponsor was Skippy Peanut Butter, and in our house, it became something of a tradition, too. It wasn't a case of the other brands not measuring up, they were simply never considered. But only creamy Skippy was acceptable. Somebody, probably my father, brought home a jar of chunky once, and it lived in the cabinet for years. Sometimes my mother would try to sneak some into a PBJ sandwich, but she never got away with it. There must be a law of nature that prevents chunky peanut butter from spoiling, 'cause that jar lasted forever.

You asked for itLife would have been truly idyllic if only I could have spent the afternoons at Bennett's. Alas, my folks said a family ought to be together at dinner time. Mom and Dad would sit at opposite ends of the big table; my brothers would be on one side and my sister, who's the oldest of the four of us, would sit next to me. She and I got along great since the only thing we had in common was a last name.

Now, any kid who's ever swished a shot from the foul line knows the best time to shoot baskets is during those special hours tucked between the end of school and the beginning of dinner. There's a kind of magic in effect at that time of day, a special something that enhances a shooter's aim, adds loft to a lay-up and takes the edge off the worst arguments about who fouled whom. As far as I can tell, it still holds true today.

Back then, the best way for me to follow up an afternoon of basketball was to watch the "Howdy Doody Show," which is why I was frequently late getting home for dinner. When I eventually got home, my mother and I would observe yet another tradition, like a responsive reading, except we both had our parts memorized.

"You're late," Mom would say.

"I know. I'm sorry," I would always respond.

"Don't they have any clocks at Bennett's house?"

"Sure, but you know, we were busy, and I sorta forgot to look."

"You didn't notice it was getting dark?"

"Well, yeah, but it gets darker earlier every day!" (After all, basketball is a winter sport, and the best time to get ready for it is in the fall. Finding a place to shoot baskets outdoors during a Minneapolis winter is tricky.)

"But if the sun goes down earlier, shouldn't that give you even more time to get home?"

"I guess."

"You're not sure?"

"Okay, you're right. I'm sorry. It won't happen again, I promise."

"I've heard that before." Which is true, I made the same promise every time. I suppose I should have said "It won't happen again, *tonight*," but I never did.

One evening, after we had observed the usual "You're late/I'm sorry" ritual, Dad made an exciting announcement: his company had been hired to produce a training film for the local Skippy Peanut

Butter factory. That was a shocker, we hadn't known there was a local Skippy Peanut Butter factory! Dad planned to make arrangements to tour the facility, which was only open to the public on Saturdays, and wondered if any of us wanted to come along. He knew the answer in advance; even my sister wanted to go! The date was set: a Saturday some four weeks off. Who knew--Art Baker himself might even be there!

I believe it was the following day, an hour or two after resuming my usual occupation in Bennett's driveway, that I really noticed how dark it was getting. I must have said something to Bennett because I remember him running to his garage, swinging his arm in a theatrical flourish and yelling "Ta-da!" just before he flipped on the newly installed floodlights. Sundown? Hah! We managed to get in at least an extra half hour. I returned home tired, but happy.

"You're late."

"I know. I'm sor--"

"Don't say it!" My mom had a stare that could freeze water coming out of a spout.

"But--"

"Don't say another word. I've heard it all anyway."

"I--"

"Shush!"

I shushed.

"Your father and I had a long talk about you. We're tired of having to track you down every night before dinner."

Track me down? Right. As if my location had ever been a mystery. But I opted not to respond as I could already feel little red chunks of ice bobbing around in my bloodstream.

"It's about time you learned some responsibility," she said. "So here's what we're going to do."

I've always had a pretty vivid imagination so it wasn't difficult to conclude that my trips to Bennett's would soon be banned.

"The next time you show up late for dinner, you're going to lose a privilege."

"A privilege? You mean like stayin' up late on a Friday night?"

"I mean like going to the Skippy factory."

"The Skippy factory?"

All of a sudden the little chunks of ice floating around in my system decided to have a team meeting at mid-court--somewhere near my heart.

"Yup," she said. I remember her voice was light, almost unconcerned, and wouldn't have been any less incongruous if she had confirmed that one of my toes was about to be removed--at about the knee.

"I won't be late again. I promise."

"Good," was all she said.

For the next two weeks, I was the most punctual child on the planet. There were times when I was even early. I figured I was storing up "earliness" like a squirrel stashing nuts for the winter.

In all fairness to Bennett, I shouldn't really blame him for what came next. While President Eisenhower was warning everybody about the "military/industrial complex" Bennett's folks went out and spent their vacation money on the entertainment industry's greatest achievement: color TV!

Somehow the magic went out of the junior-size Laker basketballs, the springboard, and the dwindling daylight. How could it possibly compete with the likes of "Crusader Rabbit," "Tom and Jerry," or "Huckleberry Hound"--in full and sometimes accurate, color? Dinnertime couldn't compete very well either. I went home late.

Mom met me at the door. "You're late."

"I know. I'm sor--"

"You know what this means, don't you?"

Even someone with extremely limited deductive powers could tell this was not a happy woman. "The Skippy trip?" I asked.

"The Skippy trip," she confirmed. "Your dinner is in the kitchen."

That's all she said! Period. She didn't ask why I was late or anything. There was no argument, no pleading, no tears, no second thoughts--nothing. And it was two whole weeks before we were going on the tour! There was no way in the world she could possibly remember I had been late that one lousy time.

If I had turned punctuality into an art form before, I became one of the "Old Masters" in the days that followed. I made sure I was home early every night, not just once in a while. I was the first one at the dinner table. I ate the liver. I even helped with the dishes when it wasn't my turn. I wagered everything I had on the value of good works to dull the memory of my earlier transgression.

The long-awaited Saturday finally arrived. The house was a bustle of activity as we all got dressed and ready. I remember helping my sister clean up after breakfast as Dad loaded the Brownie with fresh film and stuffed his pockets with little blue flash bulbs.

We all prepared to troop out to the car when Mom pulled me aside and asked, "Where do you think you're going?"

That was definitely not a question I was prepared to hear. "The Skippy factory?" I suggested.

"I don't think so," she said. "I told you what would happen if you were late one more time."

I wept. I moaned. I sobbed. I rolled my eyes so far back in my head it hurt.

I fell to the floor and actually begged. Oh, such pathos. Everyone tip-toed by me, avoiding eye contact as if it would somehow ensnare them in my guilt. No condemned man ever created a greater spectacle than I did that morning, nor was any such protest less effective.

No reprieve. Mom was a rock, her face a mask of steely resolve. While my family spent the day reveling in Skippydom, I languished in my room.

That evening I discovered I represented only half of the casualties. Rounding out the massacre was my father, the very architect of the whole affair. His undoing came when a security guard spotted his camera and leaped to the conclusion there was industrial espionage afoot.

While I sat in my room, Dad sat in the car. (When he and his film crew arrived some weeks later there was a similar scene with the same uniformed enforcer, but the outcome was entirely different. I never did get to see the training film.)

Much later, I learned there were other casualties as well, including at least a part of my childhood innocence. And despite my considerable display of grief, my mother suffered most of all. In later years she confessed that saying "no" to me that day was one of the hardest things she ever had to do.

~End~

Chapter 35

Save Your Family's Words of Wisdom

I touch on this topic often in my memoir writing classes, so it's only logical to include it here. For many of us, there are precious words of wisdom tucked away in our memories. Odd and typically quirky, these folksy lines played a subtle yet important role in our childhoods. We ignore them all too often today, because they haven't been run through a Madison Avenue filter, nor are they used by the relentlessly Mid-western broadcast voices we hear every day.

If we're lucky, we won't have much trouble digging them up to share with our own progeny. BUT, we have to commit ourselves to doing so. Memoir writers, on the other hand, have additional opportunities. They can work these gems into their personal histories and leave these verbal riches for posterity.

"Wish in one hand, spit in the other. See which fills up first."

I'm channeling the wisdom of the diminutive Anna Gunderson Hasdal, the only one of my grand quartet to survive past my third birthday. Doubtless the other three could have provided similar proverbs if they'd only had the chance, and I ache for the memories of them I'll never have.

Happily, Anna lived a long and bountiful life, and I have many great recollections of her.

Standing all of 4 foot 10 in her sensible, sturdy, little shoes, Anna left Norway at 18 and sailed to America. She shuffled through Ellis Island at the beginning of the 20th century and made her way to Chicago where she sought her fortune as a housekeeper. She met and married yet another ex-pat Norwegian, and they had four children, one of whom was my late mother.

"Gramma" was a no-nonsense gal, and I dearly wish she could share her wisdom with me and my writing classes today. She could teach me so, so much about a world which no longer exists--the one she grew up in. What she learned about that world, however, still applies to this one.

"What you don't have in your head, you have in your feet."

This one annoyed me greatly as a child, because I heard it so often. I hated it because it was true; it's still true today: forget the car keys? Walk back and get 'em; forget my class notes? Go back and get 'em. Forget the grocery list? Thankfully, parts of my memory still work, and I know I can survive without everything on the missing list. I've gotten quite a kick out of using the phrase on my own kids -- and with any luck, they'll use it on theirs, too. We'll see.

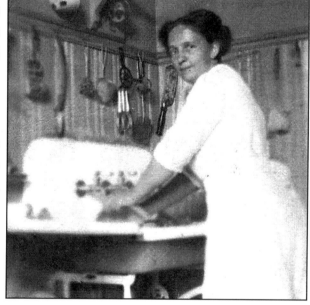

"I have more time than money."

It was true for Anna, and it's still true for me and my bride. Better still, it requires no explanation. Of course, these days she would have added some injunction about where and when to put away one's cell phone.

"I can clean up by myself, but I can't visit by myself."

If company dropped by and insisted on helping with the dishes or some other post-gathering chore, one could always count on Anna to offer the comment above.

"We don't count the food."

Anna wasn't the only one to dole out familial wisdom. This line was one of my dad's favorites. The third of five boys in his family, they shared a house with their parents plus various aunts and uncles all through the Depression. No doubt, a limited budget demanded that all food be scrupulously accounted for. As an adult, Dad no longer had such concerns, and that provides everything I need to understand.

"Chickens don't praise their own soup."

I seriously doubt my grandmother ever said this, but I can easily imagine her doing it, and I can almost hear that faint Scandinavian lilt in her voice, which was every bit as small and charming as she was. Best of all, this one takes a moment or two to absorb. And, seriously, shouldn't advice be something one has to think about to appreciate? Otherwise it's not much more than, "Be careful, or you'll shoot yer eye out!" Okay, got it. Moving on now, sans BB gun. And self respect. Here's another my great dame would surely have endorsed:

"Don't talk unless you can improve the silence."

If only our elected representatives put this to use! In lieu of that, we must do what we can, and this is prime stuff for a memoir. It'll go in mine, for sure, one way or another. Which brings me back to the beginning--spend the time it takes to dig up the sayings which got traction in your family.

"Cook 'em; don't Shermanize 'em!"

This one I remember quite vividly; it was a favorite of my late father-in-law, (and yes it refers to the Union General who burned a swath from Atlanta to Savannah). I was still in college when I began dating my future bride. Her father would dispatch us to the backyard barbecue grill on Saturday nights with the grand injunction above. Saturday night was steak night, and you didn't want to mess with that man's favorite meal. Fortunately, we didn't screw it up too often. Otherwise, I'm not sure I'd have had his blessing when I asked for permission to marry his sweet baby girl.

Please, do your best to capitalize on these things. They may help to keep alive the memories of loved ones long gone. Though the sayings may have been corny, or ungrammatical, or phrased with a degree of color rarely seen today, your memoir will benefit from them. And so will your readers.

> **Consider This:**
>
> Make a list of the pet phrases you heard when growing up. I'm not talking about the day-in, day-out sayings we've all heard. I'm referring to the special ones–those that were peculiar to your family and/or close circle of friends. You may be surprised to find new episodes to record and present. Keep those note cards handy!

~*~

Chapter 36

How to Drive Readers Away-Cover Fails

Good covers help sell books; bad ones almost never do. I say "almost" because you might find a cover are so utterly awful, amateurish or dumb that you're tempted to buy it to see if the writing is just as bad. This is like hitting your head with a variety of hard objects to see which generates the worst headache. Don't let your cover be one of them.

No matter what kind of book you're writing, a bad cover can sabotage all your hard work. If you can't think of a good illustration, a nifty font, or a way to typographically promote your idea, just use plain bold text on a color background. It might not be sexy, but at least it won't completely suck. And people will be able to read the title!

Consider the **Gummy Baby** cover at right. I have not read it, nor do I intend to, but readers of gruesome short stories featuring young children might like it. (Get your copy from Amazon.) I'm posting it simply to point out some of the issues one can run into when designing a cover.

If only you could see this cover in all its full color glory. [Sigh]

Let's start with the overwhelming background image and the photo overlay of lips and a tongue. Even assuming the mouth addition is a good idea (which I doubt), you'd be hard pressed to see it in the thumbnail version. The title also disappears amid the candy even though it's big enough to stand out. The color is just... *wrong* (though you'll have to take my word for it). The tag line likewise dissolves in the confectionery madness as it does on a full-size rendering. Last of all, the author's name is nearly invisible in a thumbnail, and doesn't do much better full-scale. The one message we can't escape is that this story has something to do with gummy bears.

Yuck.

A good book cover should deliver a message, but it ought to be one that puts an idea in a reader's head, and more specifically, an *intriguing* idea. You do, after all, want to sell what's inside, so why make the wrapper appear toxic?

Consider the cover for **Isis: The Beauty Myth** (also available at Amazon). I'm going to crawl out on a limb here and guess the cover illustration was not done by a professional artist. Conventional wisdom suggests that a pretty face, which I'm guessing is the goal here, ought to include a nose, two eyes, and maybe even an ear. Isis here, despite a charming, albeit massive, pair of ruby lips, appears to be missing some of the aforementioned standard equipment. Maybe that's the whole point of the story; I don't know. I haven't read this one either, and with this cover, I've no intention of doing so, which is sad because it might be a great story.

If I were re-designing this, I'd focus on the title font, enlarge it and find a compelling image to go with it. I'd also beef up the size of the author's name so it's not lost in the shuffle. Alas, this black and white rendition doesn't give full justice to the mauve colored background or the clash of yellow text serving as the byline.

Next up is the cover for **Bigfoot Bob** (Once again, available at Amazon). Bob Smith is Bigfoot Bob, and I'm guessing the hirsute fellow on the cover is the author rather than one of the critters he's after (or possibly a lost member of ZZ Top).

The large black box which, thankfully, obscures Bob's nether regions tells readers exactly what this wannabe blockbuster is about. Unfortunately, it's done in a font and color scheme that's barely legible full size let alone in a thumbnail, which is all most readers will see. Likewise, the image suggests this is what a bigfoot looks like rather than a bigfoot hunter. Why Bob hunts in the nude is a question for another day. This cover needs a makeover in the worst way. Sorry Bob. You, too, bigfoot.

Zipping right along, we find the cover for **Dead End in The Pyrenees** (Yep, Amazon has it). I've got to say I love the background photo. I just wish the designer hadn't quit right there. Would it have killed him or her to center the title? Or use a photo of a real Volkswagon instead of something from a freebie clip art collection? Or, at the very least, make the author's name big enough to read, and in a font that doesn't get buried in the background?

What's also interesting to note (from the Amazon sales page): this is the fourth book in a series. I have no idea if the first three covers were similarly mangled, but I suspect so. There's potential here, but all of it has been overlooked and/or misinterpreted. I also note that "Author Way" is the publisher. Evidently, they don't know squat about covers either, or they'd never have let this one sneak by. My guess is they were done the instant they got paid.

It's not that hard to come up with a good cover, even on your own. You can pay a designer to build one or use any of the cover construction tools available on the internet. I will revisit this issue in the next chapter with a list of things to keep in mind should you yearn to design your own.

> ## *Consider This:*
>
> *Paying for a book cover can be expensive. A custom designed cover consisting of front, back and spine will generally run about $500. Two or three stock photos, an alternative layout or two, and some back cover copy is typical. Lulu.com charges around $500 these days, and Createspace.com runs around $700. Ebook covers are generally much less, about $250. There are, however, any number of companies eager to root around in your wallet for a great deal more – in the thousands.*
>
> *A bad cover will hurt sales, but a great cover won't guarantee them. You can get by very well with a good cover. It doesn't have to qualify for wall space in a national gallery somewhere.*

~*~

Chapter 37
More on Covers, not Moron Covers

I know your Mom told you not to judge a book by its cover, but frankly that's absurd. If someone's browsing for a book to buy, the cover is the first thing they see. If you can't intrigue a potential reader during the nanosecond he or she devotes to your cover, you've lost a sale. *Clunk.* Done.

So, how can you make sure your cover works? Start by saving this list of suggestions and then try using them. Just remember, all of this is rule of thumb; it ain't gospel. You might be able to get away with ignoring an item or two, but chances are you'll have a better cover if you don't.

1 -- Try to find a single idea from your story to portray on the cover, then make it as compelling as possible. Give it the majority of space and importance. Don't try to drop clues about other things that happen along the way. No extra photos, no floating props, no insider messages. Stick to the main point. (I think the point of **Flightless Angels** is that some people are seriously stupid.)

You've got very little reader consideration time to work with, so your cover has to be powerful enough to instantly convey the genre, the primary focus, and the tone of your story. Is it a mystery? An epic fantasy? A memoir? A textbook? Whatever you've

written, the cover needs to make it obvious.

2 -- Chances are, you won't ever find the perfect graphic, the one that absolutely nails what you're trying to get across. But, if you're intent on using an image of some kind, find one that doesn't obscure your message. Look for a cover graphic that captures the feel of the story, whether it's bright, gloomy or something in between.

3 -- Don't overwhelm the cover with colors. Stick with a limited palette. There are a variety of them online. Take the time to review them if you aren't sure what colors work best together.

4 -- Your reader shouldn't have to guess at the title. Use large, easy-to-read letters and a font that fits the character of the work for your title. (Never use Comic Sans, as in the first example's byline.)

5 -- If you can't read the title on a thumbnail, make the title bigger. That thumbnail could be the only way your potential reader ever sees your book. Just remember that a large crappy font may be just as hard to read as a small one.

6 -- Avoid using more than two fonts, and don't put anything in all caps. You want to positively influence your potential reader. All caps means shouting. Do yourself a favor; don't shout at potential readers.

7 -- Using homegrown artwork on your cover is generally a bad idea. Avoid the temptation. Cheap clip art is not an acceptable substitute! Spend a couple bucks on good art. You won't regret it. The internet will open the door to an endless array of stock photo sellers, and most of them share a great deal of the same material.

8 -- Your best bet may be to pay a professional to design your cover. The do-it-yourself variety tend to be pretty obvious, and that's not the image you want to project.

[Note: the covers shown here are for non-existent works. I made 'em up as examples of bad covers. I can't help it if some readers might actually want to read whatever might be inside of them, but the thought makes me shudder. --Josh]

Here's a cover that works pretty well. So well, in fact, that I modeled the cover for this book after it.

~*~

Chapter 38

How 'Bout an Audio Memoir?

Let's say you've tried your best; you've done the exercises, and you've put real, honest effort into writing your memoir, but you're just not at the top of your game when it comes to grammar, punctuation and spelling. And you haven't even begun to think about how you'll format your work once you finish writing it.

You could always hire someone to do the editing and layout, but that can be expensive. Some of the so-called "publishing services" charge five to ten thousand dollars for making your story readable.

The temptation is to give up, but I sincerely hope you won't. There's another alternative to consider: audio memoir.

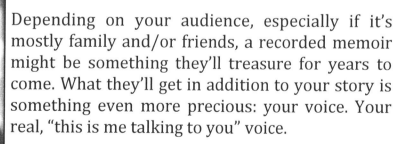

Depending on your audience, especially if it's mostly family and/or friends, a recorded memoir might be something they'll treasure for years to come. What they'll get in addition to your story is something even more precious: your voice. Your real, "this is me talking to you" voice.

I would give anything to have something like that from my parents or grandparents. They're all long gone now, and the only thing I have that even comes close is a recording my father did when he was practicing for a speech he gave to his local Toastmasters Club.

He did it with a hand-held mini-recorder, and the

sound quality was below dreadful and just slightly above useless. *But it's <u>his</u> voice!* And along with every cough, sneeze, and whisper, the sound of his voice is enough to bring me to tears. His laughter, his attitudes, and his demeanor are perfectly captured even if the quality of the recording leaves much to be desired.

I copied the recording I had and made it available to the rest of my family. Not surprisingly, they reacted the same way I did, with a mixture of joy, tears and laughter.

Do you imagine those who love you would feel any differently about a recording of your voice, telling your story?

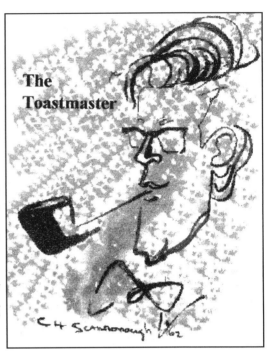

The good news is that you can start with what you've already written. You'll still have to finish it, of course, but because you'll be reading it instead of printing it, you no longer have to worry about spelling, punctuation and the finer points of grammar.

Okay then, let's assume you've decided to do an audio memoir. That's awesome. And, if you think about it, pretty darned brave, too. It's not something just anyone can do. But, before you rent time on an MGM sound stage, or get another mortgage to convert your spare bedroom into a home recording studio, it might be a good idea to do a little warm up, first. This is what folks who know mean when they say, "It's a marathon, not a sprint."

You can start with the free software that comes standard on most home computers. If you're using a machine with a built-in camera, then you've almost certainly got a built-in microphone, too. Neither may be state-of-the-art, but who cares? For now, you're just stretching and flexing.

If all you want to do is hear yourself, crank up the sound recorder

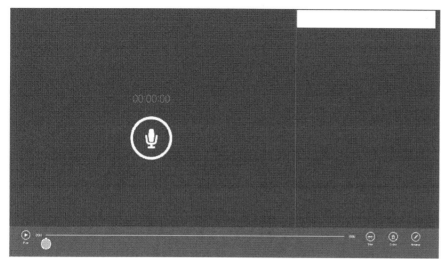

program that came with your computer. You may have to search for it, but it shouldn't be too hard to find. If you just can't find the darned thing, consider casting aside your technical shyness and ask someone who knows your PC (Mac, whatever) a little better than you do.

Don't be concerned if they smirk and tell you how miserable the built-in stuff is. Right now, that's not important. You'll eventually learn a lot about recording audio. Hey, you've got to start somewhere, right? For now, just suffer through the commentary, shoo the interloper from the room, and crank up the program. If it asks for permission to use your built-in microphone, click "Yes."

The dreadful screen above is from Windows 8.1. Sadly, the one that pops up in version 10 isn't much better. It does, however, work the same way.

You're probably looking at a screen you've never seen before. With any luck, it'll be fairly free of clutter (buttons, dials, controls and whatnot). In fact, there's probably little more than a microphone graphic on the screen. That's enough. Click on it and start talking. Feel free to yack about anything that comes to mind. It doesn't matter.

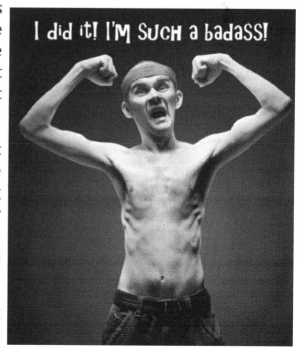

Now, while you're chatting away, notice that the dot underneath the line is moving to the right. That means you're actually recording something. It could just be the sound of your breathing, but if you're actually talking, words are being recorded! Whoa -- who knew it was that easy?

When you click on the circle symbol that replaced the microphone thingy, the recording stops. Click on the triangle in the lower left-hand corner of the screen to hear yourself. Note: it could be painful.

[Pause for sharp intake of breath]

I'm guessing one of two things just happened. Either you didn't hear anything (or it was so faint it amounts to the same thing), OR you realized your voice sucks. It's too high, or too low, too soft, or too raspy, or it sounds like someone is trying to make fun of you. Alternative One is easy to fix; just crank up the volume. Alternative Two? You'll just have to live with it. For now, anyway. Later, with better recording tools, there might be some hope.

You're not done yet, however. It's time to *read* something out loud. Maybe it's a part of your memoir, or your notes for your memoir, or maybe someone else's memoir. Whatever. Just read it and record it. Remember, we're just playing around here, trying to get used to the idea of making a recording of your voice. The likelihood that you'll want to actually use what you record now is remote -- seriously, like Easter Island remote.

When you're done, save it. Depending entirely on the freebie recording software you used, this could be a simple task, or not. Again, if you need help, ask your techie pal for it. This would also be a good time to figure out where you're going to store the stuff you intend to put into your audio memoir. While you're working on it, there are going to be many, many (did I say "many"?) audio files. You're going to need to identify them -- in order -- so when the day finally comes you'll be able to assemble them in one grand pile. Maybe with photos and charts and diagrams, too. And other sound effects. When naming your audio files, incorporate a numbering scheme. Number your audio clips in sequence, by 10's. This is in case you decide later to insert something you forgot.

F'rinstance: 10AUD-my birth; 15AUD-learning to walk; 20AUD-my 1st pet, etc.

We'll be talking soon about some really good audio recording software. Best of all, you'll be able to afford it, no matter what your budget looks like.

For now, get busy working on what you intend to record. If you're not sure where to start, try reading through the suggestions in chapter 10. If you still can't think of anything to write about, it could be a sign of something more significant. To be brutally honest -- another way to say "blunt" -- if you haven't got anything to say, why open your mouth?

> ## *Consider This:*
>
> *No matter what final form your memoir takes, getting it done requires some hard work. If an audio memoir suits your needs, then put in the time to do it right. That means writing down everything you intend to record. Use whatever spelling or punctuation works for you. No one else need ever see it! But right it down you MUST. Trying to dictate a memoir without even having notes to go by is a project doomed to failure.*
>
> *If you've gotten this far, you know you can finish, and finish properly. You owe it to yourself. Don't talk yourself out of it simply because it's going to be difficult. Life is difficult, and you've handled that!*
>
> *You CAN do this!*

~*~

Chapter 39

Audio Memoir – Part Two

Thanks to the efforts of my writer/musician/watchmaker friend, Steve Whitworth, I have the information needed to finish the topic of audio memoirs. Steve's knowledge and familiarity with the art of sound recording far exceeds anything most folk need to create a quality audio rendition of their life story. But it never hurts to heed the recommendations of a pro. And I have, so here goes....

The kind of software you'll need comes in two broad flavors. The first is browser-based, meaning that you need to go on-line and connect with a website, and do your recording there. The second option is software you download and install on your computer so you can use it anytime, without needing the internet. Which type you choose depends largely on your budget, the size of your recording project, and the quality level you'd like to achieve. Like everything else in life, there are trade-offs.

For the rest of this section, I'm going to focus on the browser-based products. We'll get to the downloadable software in the following chapter. Then, to wrap up any remaining loose ends, we'll look at affordable options for hardware to dramatically improve the quality of your recording.

The goal of our audio editor search was to find something free (or very cheap) which a user with little or no recording experience could tackle quickly and easily. There are several browser-based programs that will do the job, but two stand out above the others for simplicity and ease of use. If your internet browser is up and running, you can zip on over to **Hya-Wave** (https://wav.hya.io/#/fx) or **TwistedWave** (https://twistedwave.com/).

Both of these websites offer exactly what we were looking for: controls that mimic tape recorder buttons and very little else. The on-screen wave forms should be familiar to anyone who watches crime dramas on TV, and even if you don't, it'll quickly become clear what they represent. The downside to using these on-line programs is that you'll be limited to short duration clips--recordings of 5 minutes each.

You could digitally "glue" them together later, but that would require the use of another program, most likely one that came with your computer (both Mac and PC come with a variety of such applications) or one you'd have to download. So if you're keen on recording your memoir, there's very likely a new download in your future.

I tried both Hya-Wave and TwistedWave with the built-in microphone in my computer <u>and</u> with an auxiliary mic I plugged into a USB port. (I used a Samson C01U studio condenser mic which I bought at a guitar store a couple years back for under $100.) The difference in sound quality was, and I'm not exaggerating: *astounding*.

When I used the built-in microphone, my voice sounded muffled and indistinct. It was equally bad in both systems. Most of those issues instantly disappeared when I used the "real" microphone.

I was disappointed in the quality of the Hya-Wave recordings which slowed down in playback, and I could find no way to speed them up. The second recording, done with the auxiliary mic was better by a thousand percent, but the playback was still slow. I had no such problems with TwistedWave and therefore recommend it as the better of the two systems.

Use a "real" mic, and you'll be amazed, too.

Setting up an account with TwistedWave is free and easy. And, since you'll need a great deal more than five-minute chunks if you're going to record an entire memoir, it makes sense to pay for an upgrade. Five bucks a month buys the basic plan which allows for 20-minute files and a total of 10 hours of storage. That ought to cover most memoir projects. If not, an "advanced" package is available for ten dollars a month and provides 60-minute file capability with storage for 20 hours of recordings. If you need more than that, you obviously talk too much!

If your recording goal is to do it fast and cheap, this is the way to go. For a little more money, however, you'll get a much better result using software that's loaded directly onto your computer. We'll discuss that next time.

> ### *Consider This:*
>
> *I'm guessing that if you experimented with the recording software built into your computer, you saw how much better the browser-based programs are. If you haven't compared them, now's the time to do it!*
>
> *Get busy.*

Chapter 40
Audio Memoir-Part Three

As mentioned before, you don't need to be a professional sound engineer to create an audio memoir. You do need to be patient and persistent. You also need to be willing to learn some new skills. Thankfully, they aren't too difficult.

In the last chapter we discussed cheap recording alternatives. This time we'll look at a couple more, one of which costs a bit. But both programs take sound recording-- in terms of the experience *and* the result--to a much higher level.

Once again, I'm beholden to Steven Whitworth for his help in sorting all this out. He recommends one of two programs available on-line: **Audacity** and/or **Reaper** (both of which are available from Amazon, among other places).

Audacity is open source shareware, meaning the code is freely available to both users and developers. (Side note: a major upgrade to the Audacity code was developed by Paul Licameli who is not only a brilliant programmer, but a gifted voice-over artist as well. He single-handedly produced the amazing Audible version of my short story collection, ***Christmas Beyond the Box***, which you should rush out and buy right away!) Though Audacity is available for your use at no charge, remember that many people donated their time and expertise to create and maintain it; the least you can do is pony up a few bucks in a donation aimed at encouraging them to keep the program viable.

According to Steve, Audacity provides a well thought out setup and a thorough range of features. I can attest to that, too. I've used the program to do soundtracks for several book trailers. Below is a screen shot of Audacity in action. Try not to freak out over all the controls. It's actually less complicated than it looks. The documentation for both programs is more than adequate, and if you take your time, you should have little difficulty navigating either one.

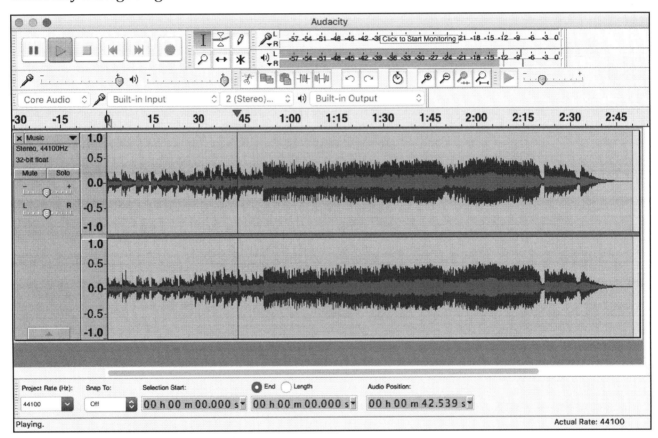

Audacity screen shot. It's not nearly as complicated as it looks!

Reaper has much more going for it than a seriously creepy name. Once again, according to Steve, it provides an excellent set-up via their virtual mixer with adequate but easy to use enhancements--features somewhat superior to those on Audacity. You'll have to pay for it, however. The standard home edition is listed on their website for $60. To my way of thinking, that's an excellent deal.

Also note: Older versions of far more sophisticated programs like Logic Pro (for Apple) and Pro-Tools (for the PC) are available for download at greatly reduced prices. The cost is in the $30-$40 range. HOWEVER, the learning curve is much steeper, and they take up a tremendous amount of space on a hard drive.

Either Audacity or Reaper will do a great job and are not much harder to use than a garden variety tape recorder. Their output can be markedly improved, however, by the use of some additional hardware, which we'll discuss in the next and final chapter on this topic.

> **Consider This:**
>
> *You've got nothing to lose in experimenting with Audacity, at least. It won't cost you anything to try it, and as my late, great grandmother always told me about trying strange, sometimes green, veggies, "You might even like it!"*

~*~

Chapter 41

Audio Memoir-Part Four

If you're not satisfied with basic, entry-level audio for your recorded memoir, then you're in good company. What, after all, is the point of putting in all the time and effort to create something if you're not going to make it as good as it can be? Especially if all that stands in the way is a modest expenditure.

You'll need a couple extra pieces of hardware if you want your work to sound more professional. Start with a decent microphone. My audio engineering friend, Steve Whitworth suggests the following:

Blue Snowball iCE--a condenser mic by famed microphone maker Blue, known for high end studio mics. It's $50 on Amazon but probably reasonably priced at your local music store, too.

Another option is the CAD U37--also a condenser. CAD is famous for tough, reliable drum mics, and this one is only $41 on Amazon, though local retailers are sure to carry it as well.

When using programs like Audacity and Reaper (see last chapter), sound quality can be elevated to the point of near professional voice-over work with the additional investment in an audio pre-amp. In recording studios, microphone signals of any and every variety are run through a "pre-amp" before being fed to a recording medium, in our case, a computer.

The job of the pre-amp is to "warm" the signal and bolster its frequency response across the spectrum. End result: the recorded voice sounds more like you, clearer, and slightly louder. This improved signal gives you more to work with in the mixing process and can enhance the listenability of voices that are not ideal for public speaking or reading projects. In other words, it makes a non-trained voice sound more like a trained one.

An excellent product for just this purpose is a Presonus Audio Box; it's a pre-amp that sports an internal digital interface. The digital interface converts your mic's output to data your computer can process. This one unit does both, extremely well, and it costs a meager $100.

If you use such a device, you'll need a traditional condenser microphone to connect to it, NOT a USB-ready style mic. Again, there are a couple bargain choices available. Steve suggests:

AudioHipster AH-01--it sells for $125 on-line at AudioHipster.com. It's a professional quality voice-over mic, and someday, when the industry figures out how good it is, the price will go up.

Option 2 is the MXL- 990--another excellent choice which we've seen locally for $69. Simply put, it's a hell of a mic for the money.

To recap, here are some Sears style option packages:

GOOD: Audacity--Free download. Works with your built in mic.

BETTER: Audacity with a USB-ready mic, like a CAD U37.

BEST: Audacity with a Presonus AudioBox pre-amp/interface for $100 and an MXL 990 mic for $69.

The very best option is only $169, and you'll sound like a pro. Not bad. If you have any recording experience, you may prefer Reaper for the more sophisticated features, in which case add $60. Still a damn good deal.

Happy recording!

Do it right. What have you got to lose?

~*~

> **Note:** *This final chapter also appears in my fiction writing textbook,* Write Naked! *It is included here because the information in it applies as much or more to memoir than to fiction. Should you choose to follow the suggestions contained herein, I believe your memoir and your readers will benefit greatly.*

Chapter 42

The More Things Change? Not So Much.

We tend to hear – and repeat – the same things over and over, and when we do, we often bestow the status of "truth" upon them, even when they may not have earned it. Thus it is with "the more things change, the more they stay the same." Fact is, it just ain't so. At least, not in my experience.

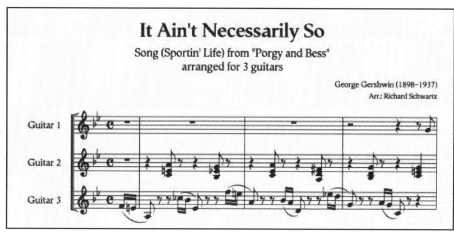

A good bit of the fiction I write is of the historical variety. I often work historical facts into contemporary stories, too. I do this sometimes for fun and sometimes because it gives readers a means to view what went on before in a different light. The same absolutely holds true for memoir writers. History can be fun, especially if, as readers, we didn't have to suffer through it.

Like many of us, I get a good deal of email that's been passed from person to person as if it were holy writ, even if the information is suspect. Snopes.com and similar sites can be helpful in verifying that. Sifting fact from fiction in the historical record sometimes requires more effort. But it cay pay off.

A couple years ago, I received an email with the following revelations, many of which I *was* (happily) able to confirm:

100 years ago:

– The average life expectancy for men in the United States was 47 years.
– Fuel for the 1914 Ford Model T (and every other gas powered vehicle) was sold in drug stores and nowhere else.
– A mere 14 percent of American homes had a bathtub.
– Only 8 percent of US homes had a telephone.
– There were only 8,000 cars and only 144 miles of paved roads.
– The maximum speed limit in most cities was 10 mph.
– The tallest structure in the world was the Eiffel Tower.
– The average US wage in 1910 was 22 cents per hour.
– The average US worker made between $200 and $400 per year.

What I found fascinating about these facts is that they suggest a setting I'd never thought about. As I read over them, my mind churned up one plot possibility after another. How could I best tap into this material and create a world my readers would enjoy? After a bit of reflection, I realized I could turn *any* of these nuggets into a story, or at least the beginning of one.

So, how does that impact memoir writers, folks who – presumably – prefer fact over fiction? I think it should impact them even more! History doesn't stop because or in spite of what we're writing. History provides the background for the lives we live. Take some time to examine what went on in the world during the time(s) you write about. A simple internet search can yield dozens, if not thousands, of topics in a single query.

It never hurts to invest a little time *now*, to help recall what went on *then*.

When I started hunting for something to illustrate item 2 in the list above, I was surprised to see three diverse interpretations. Need a hint? (They're all "T" models.)

There are plenty more stats to consider, and any of these could provide fodder for an interesting tale, or background for a memoir – all from 1914:

– A competent accountant could expect to earn $2000 per year, a dentist $2,500 per

year, a veterinarian between $1,500 and $4,000 per year, and a mechanical engineer about $5,000 per year.

– More than 95 percent of all births took place at home.

– Ninety percent of all Doctors had no college education. Instead, they attended so-called medical schools, many of which were condemned in the press and the government as "substandard."

– Sugar cost four cents a pound; coffee was fifteen. Eggs were fourteen cents a dozen.

– Most women only washed their hair once a month, and used Borax or egg yolks for shampoo.

– Canada passed a law that prohibited poor people from entering into their country for any reason.

– In 1914, the US flag had 45 stars. Here are a few more factual tidbits from that year, just in case the first batch didn't do the trick:

– The population of Las Vegas, Nevada, topped out at 30!

– Crossword puzzles, canned beer, and iced tea hadn't been invented yet.

– There was neither a Mother's Day nor a Father's Day.

– One out of every five adults couldn't read or write, and only 6 percent of all Americans had graduated from high school.

– Marijuana, heroin, and morphine were all available, over the counter, at the local corner drugstore. Back then, some pharmacists claimed, "Heroin clears the complexion, gives buoyancy to the mind, regulates the stomach and bowels, and is, in fact, a perfect guardian of health!"

– Eighteen percent of households had at least one full-time servant or domestic.

– There were about 230 reported murders in the entire US.

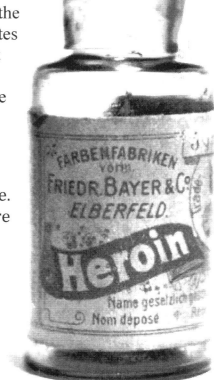

Story ideas and background color exist everywhere. You only have to expend a little effort to find more than you could possibly use.

~*~

APPENDIX

The following pages contain some very useful information, beginning with an Inventory of Life Events assembled by my good friend and fellow writer, Sonya Braverman Cooper. If you're struggling to remember events in your life, or fear you'll leave something out, take the time to review the list. You might be surprised to remember much more than you thought you could.

Another chart provides some help for those struggling to narrow down a particular emotion, or to find alternatives for emotional words you may have overused.

And finally, there are some examples of properly punctuated dialog, which seems to be a problem for a lot of people. These same examples are incorporated in my fiction writing textbook as well.

I hope you find all this helpful. I just wish I could have figured out a way to work them into one of the chapters!

Inventory of Life Events

Some life events come with every human being on the day they are born. Some are more common than others. Perhaps these items will jog some memories for you and jump start your writing. Can you think of any other events to add to the list?

Early Years
    Learning to walk and talk
    Learning how the world works
    Learning right and wrong
    Learning how to get along within and outside of the family
    Learning how to survive in the world you are born into
    Testing the boundaries of authority
    Learning to share
    Learning to tell the truth
    Making friends and enemies and learning how to tell the two apart
    Learning the norms and what is taboo in your culture

School
    Starting or finishing school
    Learning the basics
    Declining grades
    Failing a grade
    Skipping grade(s)
    Changing schools
    Dropping out of school or being dismissed

Preparing for Life
    Learning basic life skills
    Learning about who you are and who you want to become
    Learning about where you belong
    Learning about how to fit into your peer group, family, generation

Learning How to Make a Living
- Choosing a profession
- Choosing a college or trade school
- Choosing a major or area of study
- Studying, taking tests and writing term papers
- Graduating and earning a degree

Working
- Your first job
- Receiving a good/poor performance review
- Outgrowing a job and leaving
- Earning more responsibility, a promotion or a raise
- Getting a demotion
- Getting fired
- Loss of job (other than firing)
- Switching careers
- Returning to work
- Learning new skills to stay competitive
- Running your own project, department or business
- Retiring

Finances
- Change in financial status
- Major mortgage or loan
- Bankruptcy
- Bad credit
- Foreclosure of mortgage or loan
- Making a major purchase
- Saving for a child's education
- Saving for big ticket items
- Saving for retirement

Life Outside of Work
- Finding a neighborhood where you fit in
- Making a place for yourself in the community
- Buying a car and commuting to and from work
- Creating a life after work and on weekends
- Vacations
- Buying the items you need to make a home
- Creating a home
- Homelessness
- Change in residence
- Change in living conditions
- Loss or damage to personal property
- Christmas/Thanksgiving or other major holidays
- Learning about life, death and the things you value
- Learning about justice, freedom, fairness, compassion, jealousy, and competition
- Encountering obstacles and overcoming them
- Being stopped by the obstacles of life
- Learning the lessons of life
- Religion
- Fame or outstanding personal achievement

Relationships
- Falling in like and falling in love
- Dating
- Getting engaged
- Marriage or live-in relationship
- Learning how you reflect your family and early environment
- Learning to trust
- Having your heart broken
- Separation, divorce
- Relationship reconciliation
- Remarriage
- Break-up with boyfriend, girlfriend, close friend
- Infidelity
- Conflict with family members or friends
- Problems with former spouse, partner
- Social isolation
- Sexual difficulties

Confrontations with authority
Gay, lesbian and transgender issues
Non-conventional lifestyles
Trouble with in-laws
Aging parents
Work interferes with family life

<u>Children</u>

Thinking about having children, creating them, preparing for their arrival
Birth of child or multiple children
Birth of out-of-wedlock child
Raising and nurturing children
Teaching children what is accepted and what is taboo
Teaching children basic life skills
Watching children grow and participating in their life
Custody issues
Single parenting
Child leaves home
Puberty
Child abuse or neglect
Pregnancy
Stillbirth or miscarriage
Unplanned pregnancy
Abortion
Child returns home with a child
Adult child returns home to live
Physically, emotionally, cognitively handicapped child
New member of household, child or adult

Physical Health Issues
    Scraped knees and cavities
    Sniffles, colds, flu
    Surviving a health emergency
    Surviving a potentially life-threatening disease
    Illness or death of a family member or close friend
    Personal injury or illness
    Long-term hospitalization
    Mental illness of self, loved one, close friend
    Chronic pain
    Suicide attempt or completion of family member, friend, self
    Drug, alcohol, sex addiction
    Sudden accidental or violent injury or death
    Long-term chronic illness
    Serious injury, harm, or death you caused someone else
    Became disabled or incapacitated
    Learning or attention problems
    Cognitive problems
    Having a visible deformity
    Serious accident at work, home, or during recreational activity
    Exposure to toxic substance
    Physical assault or abuse
    Sexual assault, rape, incest
    Emotional abuse

Death and Dying
    Caring for, watching over and mourning the death of parents
    Caring for, watching over and mourning the death of a child
    Mourning the death of co-workers and friends
    Mourning the death of close relatives and siblings

Mid-Life Issues
    Undergoing a life-changing crisis
    Examining your life
    Thinking about past major choices and decisions
    Figuring out who you are and want to become
    Discovering what brings you happiness
    Choosing a different life path
    Menopause

Aging
- Preparing for retirement
- Deciding what to do in your "Golden Years"
- Dealing with lifestyle choices brought about by money or health issues
- Managing your property and estate

End of Life
- Preparing for disabilities and death
- Settling your affairs
- Saying goodbye to loved ones
- Experiencing dying

Other
- Legal problems
- Imprisonment
- Military service, combat or exposure to war-zone
- Natural or man-made disaster
- Captivity
- Severe human suffering
- Homicide
- Experiencing violence
- Witnessing violence
- Perpetrator or victim of crime (violent or not)

The Naked Truth

When it comes to emotion, be specific

Intensity	Happy	Sad		Angry		Scared	Confused
Strong	ecstatic elated energized enthusiastic excited exuberant jubilant loved marvelous terrific thrilled uplifted	crushed defeated dejected depressed devastated disgraced drained exhausted helpless hopeless hurt rejected terrible unloved unwanted discarded	sorrowful uncared for worthless wounded burdened condemned demoralized deserted distraught empty grievous humbled miserable mournful pitiful	abused betrayed enraged furious hateful hostile humiliated incensed outraged pissed off rebellious repulsed seething strangled vengeful	exploited fuming mad patronized repulsed spiteful throttled used vindictive	afraid appalled desperate dread fearful frantic horrified intimidated overwhelmed panicky petrified shocked terrified tormented vulnerable	baffled bewildered constricted directionless flustered stagnant trapped
Mild	admired alive amused appreciated assured cheerful confident delighted determined encouraged fulfilled grateful gratified joyful justified optimistic proud relieved resolved respected valued	ashamed despised disappointed discouraged disheartened disillusioned dismal distant distressed inadequate isolated lonely neglected slighted unappreciated upset	abandoned alienated degraded deprived disturbed drained islanded resigned slighted wasted	agitated annoyed controlled disgusted exasperated frustrated harassed infantilized irritated offended peeved resentful ridiculed smothered stifled	aggravated anguished cheated coerced deceived dominated provoked	alarmed apprehensive axed defensive guarded insecure shaken skeptical startled stunned suspicious tense threatened uneasy	ambivalent awkward disorganized doubt foggy hesitant misunderstood perplexed puzzled torn troubled
weak	content flattered fortunate glad good hopeful peaceful pleased relaxed satisfied	apathetic bad deflated disenchanted lost sorry		dismayed displeased tolerant uptight		anxious concerned doubtful impatient nervous perplexed reluctant shy timid unsure	bothered distracted surprised uncertain uncomfortable undecided unsettled unsure

Dialog Punctuation--by Example

The rules for punctuating dialog are pretty simple:

--Use quotation marks at the start and end of whatever a character says, and put all punctuation *inside* them**, even quoted dialog.

> "Holy moly, Batman--look at that car!"
> "What car?" asked the caped crusader, ignoring his companion.
> "I--"
> "That one!" Robin screamed, shouldering him aside. "It's Bat-babe! She almost ran you down."
> "--huh? No. I can't believe it." Batman adjusted his new mask; he hadn't been able to see clearly since he got it. "I'm a public servant, and according to the *Almost Daily Beagle*, 'a darned good one.'"

--Don't use quotation marks for thoughts. If a character is *thinking* (musing, considering, evaluating, etc.) put those words in italics, or use a tag to indicate it's someone's thoughts.

> *Oh, what I'd give for a chocolate sundae right now,* Homer thought.
> Somebody mentioned chocolate sundaes, and Homer palmed his face. *Oh, yummmm!*
> Homer paused. *I'd kill for a chocolate sundae right about now.* Instead, he got coffee.

--Use speech and action tags *appropriately*. Match the tag to the action.

> Wrong: "I love you," he screamed.
> Not wrong, but not great: "I love you," he moaned.
> Not great, but better: "I love you," he said, breathlessly.
> Better still: He embraced her and said, "I love you."
> Best: "I love you," he said as he revealed a 10-carat diamond engagement ring.

--Every speaker deserves a paragraph of his own.

This is just wrong:

> "John!" "Mary!" "Come away with me," he pleaded. "I can't. The children--" "Leave 'em. They're all ingrates anyway." "You can't be serious, John! They're my *children*, for God's sake." "Wake up, Mary--they're old enough to collect Social Security!"

(Besides, it looks more appealing spread out:)

> "John!"
> "Mary!"
> "Come away with me," he pleaded.
> "I can't. The children--"
> "Leave 'em. They're all ingrates anyway."
> "You can't be serious, John! They're my *children*, for God's sake."
> "Wake up, Mary--they're old enough to collect Social Security!"

**These examples are based on commonly accepted punctuation of *American* style English. In the UK, and some of the other former colonies, they follow a different set of rules. But then, many of them drive on the wrong side of the road, too. (Canadians, God bless 'em, can't make up their minds.)

~*~

Men have feelings, too.
For instance,
we feel hungry.

ABOUT THE AUTHOR

Josh Langston writes books which have amused, angered, enlightened and entertained many readers. He regularly mines history for background that's little known but reliably fascinating. His plots are complex, interconnected and layered with humor and suspense; his characters are rarely predictable, and even his bad guys tend to be both engaging and diabolical, and possibly fiendish.

Langston's readers are rarely satisfied with just one of his books, whether it's part of a series or a stand-alone. He's proud to let his southern roots show in his characters and his choice of settings.

His two most recent book releases are: **The 12,000-year-old Whisper**, a pair of oddly related love stories separated by two cultures and a dozen millenia, and **Write Naked! (The Secrets of Dynamic Prose Laid Bare)** Josh's first textbook, which provides the writing lessons schools don't offer.

The author, hard at work on his next blockbuster novel.

When he's not working on a new novel, Langston is most likely editing, teaching, blogging, or helping his wonderful wife watch their amazing grandkids. He's even been known to goof off from time to time.

You can write to him at: <u>DruidJosh@gmail.com</u> or visit his blog at **www.JoshLangston.com**.

~*~

Photo and Illustration Credits

Front and back covers: Dollarphotoclub.com

Pages 9, 10, 11, 12, 15, 16, 19, 21, 28, 29, 37, 38, 39, 41, 42, 43, 44, 46, 47, 54, 55, 56, 57, 58, 59, 60, 61, 67, 68, 70, 72, 73, 74, 75, 81, 94, 122, 126, 127, 128, 140: Dollarphotoclub.com

Page 13, 18, 19, 26, 30, 32, 34, 35, 36, 41, 50, 71, 83, 86, 91, 92, 95, 97, 98, 99, 101, 107, 108, 120, 139, 141: public domain

Page 19, 25, 27, 40, 81, 90, 96, 106, 114, 115, 116, 124, 125, 126, 127, 151, 152: Josh Langston

Page 32: nurture-clipart-jix

Page 51, 52, 63, 64, 65, 76, 78, 84, 85, 87, 88, 93, 100, 104, 105, 110, 111, 112, 123, 130, 131, 133, 136, 138, 144, 146, 148: 123rf.com

Page 102: Ancestry.com

Page 109; Hormel Foods, Inc.

Page 118: Christopher Ridge

Page 119: Shawn James

Page 120: Bob "Bigfoot Bob" Smith

Page 120: Elly Grant

Page 134: Audacity.com

Page 136: bluemic.com

Page 137: cadaudio.com

Page 137: presonus.com

~*~

Made in the USA
Middletown, DE
18 March 2017